GOD'S
FAITHFULNESS
Through Generations

Wyatt House books may be ordered through booksellers or by contacting:

WYATT HOUSE PUBLISHING
399 Lakeview Dr. W.
Mobile, Alabama 36695
www.wyattpublishing.com
editor@wyattpublishing.com

Because of the dynamic nature of the Internet, any web address or links contained in this book may have changed since publication and may no longer be valid.

Cover design by:

Interior design by: Mark Wyatt

ISBN 13:978-1-954798-14-4

Printed in the United States of America

GOD'S
FAITHFULNESS
Through Generations

by
Dr. Robert E. Morton

WHP
Wyatt House Publishing
Mobile, Alabama

What people are saying about Bobby Morton and this book...

"The exegesis of Joshua by Dr. Robert Morton is tempered with his insights by his many years of service as a pastor, evangelist, and seminary professor. By reading his book you develop a sense of how Joshua matured and was guided by the hand of God. In reading how Joshua was lead by God, this book enables us to understand how we also can depend on God daily."

Dr Steven E Bailey
Past 1st Vice President Florida Baptist Pastors Conference
Past 2nd Vice President Arkansas Baptist State Convention
Past Director of Missions Mississippi County Baptist Association,
Arkansas

"We are refreshed to follow for many years the seasons of life for gifted persons like Bobby and Mary Morton. We knew them as they prepared during their educational years. We were blessed to have them as our visitors during the years we served with IMB in Bangladesh. They had come to know international students in the University of Mobile. They developed a long friendship with a young woman from Bangladesh. In time they accepted an invitation to visit in Bangladesh.

They led the first ever seminar on Marriage Enrichment at our College of Christian Theology. They preached in many of our churches. They were well received and used of God to lead many to faith in Christ. One of their gifts is to find a place to serve wherever God places them.

The Mortons have always accepted challenges and found success in the many tasks.

They have given us a blessing by sharing of God's faithfulness in all the seasons of their fruitful lives. We hope their stories in this book will inspire all of us to be more faithful, to be God's witness wherever we are."

Thomas E. Thurman
Retired IMB Missionary, Senior Adult Minister, FBC, Columbia, MS

"Bro Bobby has given us an inspiring look into the life of Joshua and his call to leadership and action. We are challenged to examine our own call by a man who has lived out his calling from God. Bro. Bobby has served for many years as Darrell Robinson's armor bearer in *Total Church Life Ministries*. Bobby in his own right has been and continues to be a Warrior for the Lord. Many have said that Bro. Darrell has been one of the greatest soul-winners we have ever known. I can say this about Bro. Bobby Morton also. I have walked alongside this man of God enough to be able to say he, too, is a great soul-winner. You'll be inspired by what God has accomplished through His Servant."

Loren Scott Robinson, former NAMB church
planter, former Director of Missions, Clark Baptist Association, AL,
Senior Pastor of Cross Culture Church, Mobile, AL

"This book is written so well and complete with wisdom God has given Dr. Bobby Morton. The lessons in each chapter clearly explain and detail the ways of Joshua and give a parallel to how we should believe and live today. I am going to utilize the book to teach a SPORTS OUT-REACH Youth Bible Study and plan to base the lessons on the information throughout many of the chapters in the book."

Hilton Glass, Movie Ministries Outreach, Founder,
Gulf States Head Of Promotions

God's Faithfulness Through Generations is a powerful, biblical book of the great truths of God's promises and our obedience. Bobby Morton, with great insight, makes these wonderful truths come alive and show how they are a part of the daily life of a follower of Jesus. As I read it, I was blessed, encouraged, and my faith was strengthened. You will be blessed by this book!"

Dr. C. Alan Floyd
Lead Pastor, Cottage Hill Baptist Church
author of These Three: A Believer's Guide to Faith, Hope, and Love
Mobile, AL

INTRODUCTION

The faithfulness of God from creation to this very day is, without question, one of His most amazing attributes. The Creator God always keeps His Word. The Scripture tells us that He is the same yesterday, today and tomorrow. As we look at this Book written by Joshua, under the inspiration of the Holy Spirit, we see a full display of God's faithfulness to one generation.

The book of Joshua is the story of both Joshua following God's leadership and Israel as they experience God's faithfulness in conquering the Promised Land. The people miraculously crossed the Jordan River and conquered the town of Jericho. Then, with God's help again, they quickly took possession of all the main areas of Canaan.

Before Joshua died, he reminded the people to keep on loving and obeying God. Publicly, he spoke of his own willingness to serve God when he said, "And if it seem evil unto you to serve the LORD, choose you this day whom ye will serve; whether the gods which your fathers served that were on the other side of the flood, or the gods of the Amorites, in whose land ye dwell: but as for me and my house, we will serve the LORD." (24:15). The book of Joshua tells us who God is, that God is holy and jealous. Because He is holy, He is to be served and obeyed. He is God, not a man. Because He is jealous, He is to be worshiped exclusively as directed in the first of His commandments. In Exodus 20: 3, we read these words, "Thou shalt have no other gods before me."

The book also tells us what God does. He works on behalf of His people. He fought for Israel, driving out their enemies before them.

In his book, Joshua tells us what we are to do. Joshua calls God's people to serve Him in sincerity and truth. God expects genuine obedience and faithful service from His people. This book gives us an example of a man of faith.

By loving and obeying God, Joshua was able to experience the wonderful faithfulness of God in his life. We can experience the same faithfulness by loving and obeying God. "Have not I commanded thee? Be strong and of a good courage; be not afraid, neither be thou dismayed: for the LORD thy God is with thee whithersoever thou goest" (1:9). What a wonderful promise to hold on to each and every day of our lives.

It is my prayer and desire that as you study this book of God's faithfulness that this will excite, encourage and build enthusiasm in your daily walk with God and that through your obedience to God, you will accomplish God's purpose for your life.

CHAPTER 1

CHANGING OF THE GUARD

1. A LOOK TOWARD THE FUTURE

Can you imagine for a moment a person of influence in your life that has been a mentor? You have respected this person for their support and encouragement for years. Suddenly they disappear from existence by death, move to an area that is unreachable, or even are hit with a severe case of dementia with no recognition of you. How do you go ahead in life without this person that has been there for you when there were questions. I have experienced this in my life. This happened to me as I needed answers, and they were not there anymore to help me in my decisions. This is what Joshua was hit with when Moses died, and he now had the responsibility to lead the nation of Israel.

Thinking about the future is stressful for many people. Most have questions but few answers. Joshua gives some insights to prepare us for the future.

Joshua knew the past. Joshua had many years of training for leadership. He studied under one of the best known leaders in the Bible, a man named Moses. Joshua had seen Moses at his best and at his worst. He had seen miracles that flowed from Moses' staff that were given under God's direction. Now his friend and mentor was dead: "Now after the death of Moses the servant of the LORD it came to pass, that the LORD spake unto Joshua the son of Nun, Moses' minister, saying, Moses my servant is dead" (Joshua 1:1-2a). Joshua had followed Moses' leadership as he watched the children of Israel move from bondage in Egypt to their present location of travels which was near the Jordan River. The journey was to continue on with Joshua leading this multitude of people. God had prepared Joshua to lead and the people to follow his leadership.

Just as God had prepared Joshua for the tasks ahead, God prepares each of us for what He has in store for us. He never sends us out to do work of His without preparing us for the occasion. Many times we feel so inadequate, but we must remember that we are more than conquerors though Christ. (Rom 8:37b)

Joshua appreciated the present and its opportunities. Joshua looked through the problems they faced to the potential the children of God would be for His Kingdom's work. We must not focus on the circumstances of today that are negative and allow defeat, but look beyond to the promises of God. Joshua was focused, and we must do the same in order to accomplish His purpose in our lives. Joshua looked forward to the future. Joshua knew Israel's future lay in obedience to God. God commanded Joshua and the people to cross the Jordan River and to possess the land. "Now therefore arise, go over to this Jordan, thou, and all this people, unto the land which I do give to them, even to the children of Israel" (Joshua 1:2b).

God had already given the land to the people of Israel. God had provided for their needs.

God also gives us what and all we need in order to serve Him. He does this not because we deserve it but so He can accomplish His purposes through us. This was the case with Israel. As God had promised Moses, He also promised to Joshua: "Every place that the sole of your foot shall tread upon, that have I given unto you, as I said unto Moses. From the wilderness and this Lebanon even unto the great river, the river Euphrates, all the land of the Hittites, and unto the great sea toward the going down of the sun, shall be your coast" (Joshua 1:3-4). The verb tense indicates that though the land remained to be taken by the Hebrews, it was as good as theirs' since this was in God's divine purpose. God promised a great land to the people of Israel.

For a people who had been slaves and without resources, the promise of such land must have seemed only a dream. However, God promised Joshua all anyone could ask for. God promised that He would never fail or forsake Joshua and that no one would prevail against him. "There shall not any man be able to stand before thee all the days of thy life; as I was with Moses, so I will be with thee; I will not fail thee, nor forsake thee. Be strong and of a good courage; for unto this people shalt thou divide for an inheritance the land, which I sware unto their fathers to give them" (Joshua 1:5-6).

Like the children of Israel we need nothing more than God's promise. The future may seem dark and lonely, but God promises to stand with us. God's command to Joshua for the people was to be obedient to His Word: "Only be thou strong and very courageous, that thou mayest observe to do according to all the law, which Moses my servant commanded thee: turn not from it to the right hand or to the left, that thou mayest prosper whithersoever thou goest. This book of the law shall not depart out of thy mouth; but thou shalt meditate therein day and night, that thou mayest observe to do according to all that is written therein: for then thou shalt make thy way prosperous, and then thou shalt have good success. Have not I commanded thee? Be strong and of a good courage; be not afraid, neither be thou dismayed: for the LORD thy God is with thee whithersoever thou goest" (Joshua 1: 7-9).As Joshua looked toward the future, he saw that God would be with him. God promised to go before him and to protect him.

If we look back over our lives, we probably can see how God has been at work in our lives. If we will look toward the future and especially to areas of our lives where we can obey God, we will have the same assurance as

Joshua: God is already at work to carry out His purposes.

2. *A WORD FOR THE FUTURE*

Three times God commanded Joshua to be strong and courageous. We see this recorded in verses six, seven and nine. God called for Joshua's obedience. If he used all his strength to obey the Lord, Joshua would courageously lead the people of Israel into Canaan. God previously had promised to deliver the people and to lead them into the land. More than anything else the people needed a leader who would obey and trust the Creator God who would provide them the victory.

We need to consider our situation. We do not really need more technology or gadgets or more places to go or things to do. We need to follow the plan of God that endures through all generations.

The Word of God is as plain to us today as it was to Joshua then. God commanded Joshua to be "strong and courageous." We can be strong and courageous by doing exactly what God wanted of Joshua. We can use all our strength to obey the Lord and courageously do what He asks of us. This means following God's plan for our lives. In Christ, God has given us the victory. We simply need to be strong and courageous in following His will for us.

This includes being strong and courageous, involved, and obeying God's commands. It still involves doing what God wants. It means having the courage to follow God. Many people model their lives after some contemporary person or group. However, it does not make sense to follow failed models. It makes more sense to follow the perfect Model God has provided in His Son Jesus Christ.

God also promised Joshua that following His directions would lead to success. The promise was certain because God is the Lord of history. He promised to give the people the land. He gave instructions concerning how to take it. "Then Joshua commanded the officers of the people, saying, Pass through the host, and command the people, saying, Prepare you victuals; for within three days ye shall pass over this Jordan, to go in to possess the land, which the LORD your God giveth you to possess it. And to the Reubenites, and to the Gadites, and to half the tribe of Manasseh, spake Joshua, saying, Remember the word which Moses the servant of the LORD commanded you, saying, The LORD your God hath given you rest, and hath given you this land. Your wives, your little ones, and your cattle shall remain in the land which Moses gave you on this side Jordan; but ye shall pass before your brethren armed, all the mighty men of valour, and help them; Until the LORD hath given your brethren rest, as he hath given you, and they also have possessed the land which the LORD your God giveth them: then ye shall return unto the land of your possession, and enjoy it, which Moses the LORD'S servant gave you on this side Jordan toward the sunrising" (Joshua 1: 10-15). Only disobedience would hinder this success.

We need to think about our priorities and what we are doing in our lives. Since God has given us a pattern for successful living, nothing should hinder our success in life. Only disobedience can keep a person from a life of meaning and significance.

God's words to Joshua mirror at least two ideas of Psalms 1. God wanted Joshua to meditate on the law day and night. Next He indicated the godly person would prosper.

God wants His Word to be a part of our lives continuously, "day and night." When we do so, He will make our way prosperous in all we do. This is not to be mistaken in more possessions here, but building up heavenly treasures.

3. PREPARATION FOR THE FUTURE

After God spoke to Joshua concerning the future, Joshua began the process of preparing for the days ahead. Preparation is essential to achieving victory.
After describing what he had done in successfully preparing for the entrance tests to the U. S. Military Academy, General Douglas MacArthur wrote, "When the marks were counted, I led. My careful preparation had repaid me. It was a lesson I never forgot. Preparedness is the key to success and victory."1. *Memoirs*

Joshua knew the necessity of preparation in God's service. Obviously the first step in preparing to serve God is to become a Christian. Joshua shows us we need to prepare to obey God. Nothing is more important in helping us obey God than making preparation to do so!

4. OBEDIENCE FOR THE FUTURE

Joshua 1:12-18 records conversations among the people of Israel concerning the commitment of the Reubenites, Gadites, and the half-tribe of Manasseh to help take the remainder of the land, which was east of the Jordan River. These tribes enjoyed a rest at possessing the land that the people west of the Jordan would not know for years. They covenanted with the other tribes, however, to follow through on their commitment. When the conquest was complete, these men then would return to their families across the river.

These people wanted to follow God. They knew the Lord would give the victory. While Joshua's leadership was important, God's leadership was vital. They would go anywhere Joshua led as long as he followed God: "And they answered Joshua, saying, All that thou commandest us we will do, and whithersoever thou sendest us, we will go. According as we hearkened unto Moses in all things, so will we hearken unto thee: only the LORD thy God be with thee, as he was with Moses. Whosoever he be that doth rebel against thy commandment, and will not hearken unto thy words in all that thou commandest him, he shall be put to death: only be strong and of a good courage" (Joshua 1: 16-18). God's leadership is just as vital for us. God calls people to ministry to communicate His directions for our lives as we serve our Lord. We must pray for our Sunday School teachers, church staff, church leaders, pastors as they prepare for us each week.It is just as important for us to pray and study the Word of God each day to be prepared to face the things of this world and be prepared to stand boldly for our Lord. If we follow God, we can face anything with courage and confidence. God does show Himself faithful to all that are obedient to His will.

CHAPTER 2

Who's That Peeping In My Window

The transition of leadership has taken place. Joshua had now taken the lead and was ready to move ahead under God's leadership. He knew that his job was enormous and knew he must trust God for His guidance. He realized that he must survey the land he was about to lead the children of Israel into. Joshua sent spies into the land to determine the best point of entry and attack. Joshua was familiar with spying, since he was once a spy himself. He wanted to know everything about the enemy. "And Joshua the son of Nun sent out of Shittim two men to spy secretly, saying, Go view the land, even Jericho. And they went, and came into an harlot's house, named Rahab, and lodged there" (Joshua 2:1).

God never ceases to amaze me at how He uses the most unlikely people for the most unusual projects to accomplish the most unbelievable purposes. Here God uses Rahab whose profession is that of a prostitute. Who would have even thought that God could use someone like her? The Bible is filled with examples of people we might see as unfit for service for our Lord. Maybe now is the time to take a glance at some of the most unlikely people God chose to use in the Bible. A man by the name of Noah comes to mind first of all. He was a social outcast. Noah was one that did not fit in with people because he chose to do things different from everyone else. His belief system was totally different in that he was committed to doing things God's way.

Next, is a man by the name of Abram. Abram was the son of a set of parents that were out right heathens. His mother and dad both had bad lifestyles. They were swindlers and thieves.

Following was a man by the name of Moses. He grew up in the wrong country and had a speech problem. On top of that, he was raised in a dysfunctional home.

Our next candidate is a young lad by the name of David. The Israelites were about to be attacked by a giant Philistine from Gath whose name was Goliath. Saul was king and was afraid as was all the Israelite army. Nobody would stand up against the giant except David who was not a soldier but a little shepherd boy.

There are many more examples in the Old Testament that we could note here, but we will move on to the New Testament. In Matthew 4, we meet four smelly fishermen by the names of Peter, Andrew, James, and John. These were not even good fishermen because Jesus had to give them instructions on the proper time to fish. Another gentleman by the name of Matthew was probably the most disliked person on the face of the earth. He was a tax collector. Matthew was a swindler of people's money and property. He was a thief, to put it very bluntly. The next is a man by the name of Paul, a well-educated person. He belonged to the special social organizations. He sounds good so far, except he did everything possible to destroy the church. That was his mission.

The last person is a carpenter's son. He was born in a city named Bethlehem. It was well known to be a poor community. People here were not generally the most accepted in society. Jesus did not attend the right schools. His earthly parents were not the type that would be accepted in church except to pay their annual tithe. The Bible gives many more examples of people that are the lest likely to be used by God.

The presence of strangers in the house of such a person as Rahab would not be unusual and would not raise suspicion. Because of her profession, she probably would be very knowledgeable about public affairs. Her knowledge would be of a great advantage to the spies to communicate the ability of the people to wage war. As the spies enter the village, they come to the house of Rahab although not undetected. "And it was told the king of Jericho, saying, Behold, there came men in hither tonight of the children of Israel to search out the country. And the king of Jericho sent unto Rahab, saying, Bring forth the men that are come to thee, which are entered into thine house: for they come to search out all the country" (Joshua 2:2-3). The king was aware of the presence of spies and of their mission. Rahab certainly knew of the danger of such action, yet she chose to obey the Holy Spirit of God in protecting these men. God chooses to protect us in ways and places we do not understand. Certainly this would not have been the obvious choice of a place for protection while spying. "4 Then the woman took the two men and hid them. So she said, "Yes, the men came to me, but I did not know where they were from. 5 And it happened as the gate was being shut, when it was dark, that the men went out. Where the men went I do not know; pursue them quickly, for you may overtake them." 6 (But she had brought them up to the roof and hidden them with the stalks of flax, which she had laid in order on the roof.)" (Joshua 2:4-6). God had given Rahab an unusual project. Here we see God's faithfulness expressed by giving these men protection in an hour of need.

Our Lord has chosen the most unlikely to accomplish the most miraculous. Sometimes we wonder how God could use us to accomplish things that seem so far beyond what we can imagine. He just wants a willing vessel. Are we willing to make ourselves available to be used by our Lord?

I remember the night I said OK to the Lord that I would go anywhere He would send me. Months past and nothing opened for me to go anywhere. I thought that God was going to just continue to use me here near my home. Suddenly a door of opportunity opened for me to travel to another area and share to a group of pastors. I never dreamed of all the places He would send me nor of how He would use me to share with so many people over these many years now. My thought here is that if a person will allow God to use him or her, He will.

Next, we see Rahab sending the King's men in the direction of the river to search for the spies. "And the men pursued after them the way to Jordan unto the fords: and as soon as they which pursued after them were gone out, they shut the gate" (Joshua 2:7). I am always in awe of the peace that God gives as we follow His will even in trying circumstances like this. "And before they were laid down, she came up unto them upon the roof; And she said unto the men, I know that the LORD hath given you the land, and that your terror is fallen upon us, and that all the inhabitants of the land faint because of you. For we have heard how the LORD dried up the water of the Red sea for you, when ye came out of Egypt; and what ye did unto the two kings of the Amorites, that were on the other side Jordan, Sihon and Og, whom ye utterly destroyed" (Joshua 2:8-10). The problem many people have in life is believing and accepting the word of God. Here we have an example of a common harlet that has heard of the works of God and believes them. She does not question, only accepts the word of testimony and believes.

"And as soon as we had heard these things, our hearts did melt, neither did there remain any more courage in any man, because of you: for the LORD your God, he is God in heaven above, and in earth beneath"(Joshua 2:11). God's promise of his presence in our lives is a constant comfort. God had chosen Rahab to give the spies the very information they are looking for to share with Joshua on their return that will encourage the children of Israel of God's provisions. Sometimes God uses the most unusual way to convey His message to us. He gives us the command to be sensitive to His direction and discerning for the truth. We can always tell the truth by how it measures with the Word of God.

Rahab makes her request, "Now therefore, I pray you, swear unto me by the LORD, since I have showed you kindness, that ye will also show kindness unto my father's house, and give me a true token: And that ye will save alive my father, and my mother, and my brethren, and my sisters, and all that they have, and deliver our lives from death"(Joshua 2:12-13). God has instructed us to make our request known to Him. He already knew her needs just as He knows ours. He cares for us. His desire was for her best just as His desire is for our best.

"And the men answered her, Our life for yours, if ye utter not this our business. And it shall be, when the LORD hath given us the land, that we will deal kindly and truly with thee. Then she let them down by a cord through the window: for her house was upon the town wall, and she dwelt upon the wall. And she said unto them, Get you to the mountain, lest the pursuers meet you; and hide yourselves there three days, until the pursuers be returned: and afterward may ye go your way. And the men said unto her, We will be blameless of this thine oath which thou hast made us swear. Behold, when we come into the land, thou shalt bind this line of scarlet thread in the window which thou didst let us down by: and thou shalt bring thy father, and thy mother, and thy brethren, and all thy father's household, home unto thee. And it shall be, that whosoever shall go out of the doors of thy house into the street, his blood shall be upon his head, and we will be guiltless: and whosoever shall be with thee in the house, his blood shall be on our head, if any hand be upon him. And if thou utter this our business, then we will be quit of thine oath which thou hast made us to swear. And she said, According unto your words, so be it. And she sent them away, and they departed: and she bound the scarlet line in the window. And they went, and came unto the mountain, and abode there three days, until the pursuers were returned: and the pursuers sought them throughout all the way, but found them not" (Joshua 2: 14-22). She knew the area and the direction of travel for their safety. God directs us in a path of safety. We must be sensitive to the Holy Spirit as He directs our paths.

"So the two men returned, and descended from the mountain, and passed over, and came to Joshua the son of Nun, and told him all things that befell them: And they said unto Joshua, Truly the LORD hath delivered into our hands all the land; for even all the inhabitants of the country do faint because of us" (Joshua 2: 23-24). This is a testimony of encouragement during a time of need. God always provides us with encouragement in the time of our need. As we read His Word and seek His face in prayer, the circumstances of life seem to evaporate.

God chose Noah for the unbelievable purpose of

providing an avenue for the continuation of mankind, beasts, fowls and fish of the sea after the flood. God basically wanted to start over in His relationship with His creation.

God elected Abram to be a father to show His power was not contained by the principles of knowledge system. God's unbelievable purpose was to show us a man of faith.

God showed His unbelievable purpose through Moses as he was able to speak to the Pharoah and see God's chosen people released from bondage in Egypt.

David was called "a man after God's heart." He defeated the giant and later became the king. He followed Saul who was king during David's adventure with the giant.

The four fishermen and the tax collector along with a few others became the disciples of Jesus. They were later commissioned to carry on the work of our Lord as Apostles.

Paul was given the unbelievable tasks of writing under the inspiration of the Holy Spirit the majority of the New Testament.

Jesus came with the unbelievable purpose of taking on the sins of the world. He shed His blood for you and me. He was placed in a tomb and was raised on the third day to show us that we can have victory over death.

Do you feel like God could never use you because of whatever excuse you are holding on to? Well, think again about that because He can use you if you are willing to obey Him. He always prepares the most unlikely people for the most unusual projects for the most unbelievable purposes. What is He calling you to do today? What changes do you need to make in order to be completely committed to our Lord Jesus Christ?

CHAPTER 3

Does Obedience Matter?

W e have all heard the old saying that what goes around comes around and then in Gal. 6:7 *Do not be deceived, God is not mocked; for whatever a man sows, that he will also reap.* We must be careful with what we do.

Dr. David Jeremiah said in his devotional on Spiritual Laws: All of our actions in life move us in one of two directions: toward God or away from God. Our actions either result in God's blessing or God's discipline.

In Joshua 3:7-8 we see these words: *And the Lord said to Joshua, "This day I will begin to exalt you in the sight of all Israel, that they may know that, as I was with Moses, so I will be with you. 8You shall command the priests who bear the ark of the covenant, saying, 'When you have come to the edge of the water of the Jordan, you shall stand in the Jordan.*

Sometimes we come to what I call crossroads in life where we need to make decisions. Sometimes we are hindered by circumstances in making the right decision.

As we look at the position of the children of Israel at this moment, they have moved from being enslaved in Egypt. They traveled the forty year journey through the wilderness. They have arrived at the edge of the Jordan River with the Promise Land in front of them, with the Egyptian army behind them, and the river in front of them is at flood stage. They are trapped on each side by mountains with only two options. Face this army or obey God. We need to seek God for His direction in every decision we make. His plan will give us direction. All we have to do is follow His will for our lives.

I would like for us to look at some Biblical Examples of Disobedience and the Consequences:

In Gen. 2:15-17, God's command was simple and direct. Then the Lord God took the man and put him in the garden of Eden to tend and keep it. 16And the Lord God commanded the man, saying, "Of every tree of the garden you may freely eat; 17but of the tree of the knowledge of good and evil you shall not eat, for in the day that you eat of it you shall surely die."

They had everything they could ever need in the garden without the fruit of this one tree. Sometimes we think like some of the cows growing up. We think the weeds on the other side of the fence is what we want instead of the healthy grass on the inside of the pasture. Satan often tries to lure us away from following God and His will as he did with Adam and Eve. We must be faithful in obeying God in every area of our lives.

Just the next page over we find another example. Gen. 3: 6-12, 6 So when the woman saw that the tree was good for food, that it was pleasant to the eyes, and a tree desirable to make one wise, she took of its fruit and ate. She also gave to her husband with her, and he ate. 7 Then the eyes of both of them were opened, and they knew that they were naked; and they sewed fig leaves together and made themselves coverings. 8 And they heard the sound of the Lord God walking in the garden in the cool of the day, and Adam and his wife hid themselves from the presence of the Lord God among the trees of the garden. 9 Then the Lord God called to Adam and said to him, "Where are you?" 10 So he said, "I heard Your voice in the garden, and I was afraid because I was naked; and I hid myself." 11 And He said, "Who told you that you were naked? Have you eaten from the tree of which I commanded you that you should not eat?" 12 Then the man said, "The woman whom You gave to be with me, she gave me of the tree, and I ate." This is Adam and Eve using the blame game. We began here, as they like many of us, want to point the finger at someone else.

I was watching as some children were playing together and suddenly something happened and when the accident occurred, they were blaming each other. Politics is filled with this blaming someone else. It is never their fault. Sometimes we have the tendency to attempt to make excuses for our actions instead of taking responsibility and asking God to forgive us.

Here in Gen. 3:16-19 we read of the consequences of their actions. To the woman He said:"I will greatly multiply your sorrow and your conception; In pain you shall bring forth children; Your desire shall be for your husband, And he shall rule over you." 17Then to Adam He said, "Because you have heeded the voice of your wife, and have eaten from the tree of which I commanded you, saying, 'You shall not eat of it': "Cursed is the ground for your sake In toil you shall eat of it All the days of your life. 18 Both thorns and thistles it shall bring forth for you, And you shall eat the herb of the field. 19In the sweat of your face you shall eat bread Till you return to the ground For out of it you were taken; For dust you are And to dust you shall return." Women have born the pain of child birth since this garden experience and mankind has had to work hard since that time. That has been a long time of dealing with the consequences of denying the authority of an Almighty God. Adam and Eve were placed in a perfect place to enjoy the cool of the garden and the presence of God. What a price to pay for all of us. This should make us aware of just how much sin is displeasing to a Holy God.

Gen. 19:15-17 In God's message to Lot: When the morning dawned, the angels urged Lot to hurry, saying, "Arise, take your wife and your two daughters who are here, lest you be consumed in the punishment of the city." 16And while he lingered, the men took hold of his hand, his wife's hand, and the hands of his two daughters, the Lord being merciful to him, and they brought him out and set him outside the city. 17So it came to pass, when they had brought them outside, that he said, "Escape for your life! Do not look behind you nor stay anywhere in the plain. Escape to the mountains, lest you be destroyed." It always amazes me just how simple the instructions of our Lord are for those of old and for us today.

Consequences: GEn. 19:26 But his wife looked back behind him, and she became a pillar of salt. God had warned them about looking back and Lot's wife could not resist looking back and what a cost for disobedience. We cannot turn the hands of time back and so there is no reason to look back. We must look at what is here and now and to what we have ahead.

Another example is found in Ex. 2:1-4 of God's Word for Moses. And the Lord spoke to Moses, "Go to Pharaoh and say to him, 'Thus says the Lord: "Let My people go, that they may serve Me. 2But if you refuse to let them go, behold, I will smite all your territory with frogs. 3So the river shall bring forth frogs abundantly, which shall go up and come into your house, into your bedroom, on your bed, into the houses of your servants, on your people, into your ovens, and into your kneading bowls. 4And the frogs shall come up on you, on your people, and on all your servants."

Again simple instructions from our Lord to Moses. Moses went to Pharaoh and he would not yield to the message from God. So Pharaoh slept with the frogs, and in case you are wondering, this is not my idea of a good night's rest. Things only got worse for Pharaoh and the Egyptian people as he refused to let God's people leave Egypt. God will do what ever is necessary to get our attention. Pharaoh got to see God's full circle of plagues God had prepared for him.

In Lev. 10:1-4, Aaron's sons, then Nadab and Abihu, each took his censer and put fire in it, put incense on it, and offered profane fire before the Lord, which He had not commanded them. 2So fire went out from the Lord and devoured them, and they died before the Lord. 3And Moses said to Aaron, "This is what the Lord spoke, saying: 'By those who come near Me I must be regarded as holy; And before all the people I must be glorified.'"

So Aaron held his peace as Nadab and Abihu went up in smoke for their disregard for the authority of God. There are a lot of people around us living reckless life styles, and we must lovingly warn them. We must be careful that we are not caught in the hand of wrath of our God. What an opportunity we have to pray for those we encounter who are living lives openly in opposition to the Lord's will.

In Num. 20: 7-12, Moses was to speak to the rock and instead struck the rock. Then the Lord spoke to Moses, saying, 8"Take the rod; you and your brother Aaron gather the congregation together. Speak to the rock before their eyes, and it will yield its water; thus you shall bring water for them out of the rock, and give drink to the congregation and their animals." 9So Moses took the rod from before the Lord as He commanded him. 10And Moses and Aaron gathered the assembly together before the rock; and he said to them, "Hear now, you rebels! Must we bring water for you out of this rock?" 11Then Moses lifted his hand and struck the rock twice with his rod; and water came out abundantly, and the congregation and their animals drank. 12Then the Lord spoke to

Moses and Aaron, "Because you did not believe Me, to hallow Me in the eyes of the children of Israel, therefore you shall not bring this assembly into the land which I have given them."

In Josh. 1, we see Moses is dead at the point of about to enter the promise land just as God had said. The people said, "We need to be careful how we respond to our Lord." In Josh 6:18-19, is God's instruction to Joshua and the children of our Lord. 18And you, by all means abstain from the accursed things, lest you become accursed when you take of the accursed things, and make the camp of Israel a curse, and trouble it. 19But all the silver and gold, and vessels of bronze and iron, are consecrated to the Lord; they shall come into the treasury of the Lord." Here we see simple instructions with a strong warning for Israel. When we read through God's Word seeing instructions for our lives, it is a must that we obey them exactly as He says that we may avoid the judgement of a righteous God we serve. When we are disobedient, our joy in the Lord is stolen away by our cnemy called Satan. We have Holy Spirit power living inside of us to stand against the evils of this world.

In Josh. 7:15, God's Judgement reads, Then it shall be that he who is taken with the accursed thing shall be burned with fire, he and all that he has, because he has transgressed the covenant of the Lord, and because he has done a disgraceful thing in Israel. Our Lord is a righteous judge and judges those those who reject His commands. So many times we feel like those committing evil are not being watched by our Lord, but He is recording every action. We can be assured that they will pay the price one day.

In Josh 7:19-21, we see Achan's confession. Now Joshua said to Achan, "My son, I beg you, give glory to the Lord God of Israel, and make confession to Him, and tell me now what you have done; do not hide it from me." 20And Achan answered Joshua and said, "Indeed I have sinned against the Lord God of Israel, and this is what I have done: 21When I saw among the spoils a beautiful Babylonian garment, two hundred shekels of silver, and a wedge of gold weighing fifty shekels, I coveted them and took them. And there they are, hidden in the earth in the midst of my tent, with the silver under it."— Achan was stoned to death, his family and all their possession were destroyed. We see here how one person's sin affects others. What a terrible price to pay for being greedy. Scriptures tell us that our sins will find us out. There is nothing hidden. 1 John 1:9 tells us if we confess, He will forgive us. Sometime we need to have a check up to make sure we have no unconfessed sins in order for us to maintain that right fellowship with our Lord.

In Jonah 1: v.2, God's Instruction again were simple and to the point. "Arise, go to Nineveh, that great city, and cry out against it; for their wickedness has come up before Me." The people of Nineveh were his neighbors and he was very much aware of their wickedness. Jonah wanted no part of going there to share God's message. He marched off in the opposite direction running from God, which by the way, never works. Sometimes we have found ourselves trying to avoid following God's plan. We see many examples of this throughout the Bible as well as maybe a few in our own lives. Jonah spent 3 days in an acid tank (the belly of a giant fish) in order for God to get his attention. The Lord has His ways of getting our attention to do His will.

Lastly of this group is an account of a religious couple in Acts 5:1-11---Ananias and Sapphira who gave a partial offering. 1 Now a man named Ananias, together with his wife Sapphira, also sold a piece of property. 2 With his wife's full knowledge he kept back part of the money for himself, but brought the rest and put it at the apostles' feet. 3 Then Peter said, "Ananias, how is it that Satan has so filled your heart that you have lied to the Holy Spirit and have kept for yourself some of the money you received for the land? 4 Didn't it belong to you before it was sold? And after it was sold, wasn't the money at your disposal? What made you think of doing such a thing? You have not lied to men but to God." 5 When Ananias heard this, he fell down and died. And great fear seized all who heard what had happened. 6 Then the young men came forward, wrapped up his body, and carried him out and buried him. 7 About three hours later his wife came in, not knowing what had happened. 8 Peter asked her, "Tell me, is this the price you and Ananias got for the land?" "Yes," she said, "that is the price." 9 Peter said to her, "How could you agree to test the Spirit of the Lord? Look! The feet of the men who buried your husband are at the door, and they will carry you out also." 10 At that moment she fell down at his feet and died.

Then the young men came in and, finding her dead, carried her out and buried her beside her husband. 11 Great fear seized the whole church and all who heard about these events.

I have been blessed and led to preach through this passage a number of times in different churches through the years. Some interesting takeaways from this passage are that the church was growing and thriving. People were being saved and encouraged in the church. They were having great fellowship, Bible studies, praying together, unity in the body of believers and meeting needs Wow, how awesome and exciting to be a part of this 1st century church, even with a couple like this in the church!

The devil is always lurking around and looking for someone or some way to break up or disrupt what God is doing. Here we see that the devil uses this couple to hold back part of their tithe. In my messages about this very thing that happened here, I have asked the question: How many people would there be funerals for within the next week for some sitting right here today who were guilty of the same thing if God were to impose the same judgement today? In verse 11 we see the impact it had on the church. Let us not be guilty of holding back from our Lord. He always provides for His children. Remember, He has promised to meet all our needs and He is faithful to meet all our needs. Remember, we can never out-give God.

Examples of Obedience and the Rewards

In Gen. 6:5-8, we are introduced to a man named Noah. Then the Lord saw that the wickedness of man was great in the earth, and that every intent of the thoughts of his heart was only evil continually. 6And the Lord was sorry that He had made man on the earth, and He was grieved in His heart. 7So the Lord said, "I will destroy man whom I have created from the face of the earth, both man and beast, creeping thing and birds of the air, for I am sorry that I have made them." 8But Noah found grace in the eyes of the Lord.

When I look at our world today, I wonder how far we are from the days of Noah. This is the account of God's wrath on the world. He brought on a flood for forty days and forty nights. The rest of the world was destroyed by the flood as Noah took his family on the first family cruise. Noah was being obedient to God as everyone else was being disobedient to God. If we expect God's blessing on our lives, we must not look at the world's actions, but to what it is that pleases our Lord. As we are doing those things that are pleasing Him, we can be assured that blessings will follow.

A second account that I have chosen comes to us in Gen. 22:11-13 showing God's provision for Abraham as he demonstrates obedience to a Holy God. But the Angel of the Lord called to him from heaven and said, "Abraham, Abraham!" So he said, "Here I am." 12And He said, "Do not lay your hand on the lad, or do anything to him; for now I know that you fear God, since you have not withheld your son, your only son, from Me." 13Then Abraham lifted his eyes and looked, and there behind him was a ram caught in a thicket by its horns. So Abraham went and took the ram, and offered it up for a burnt offering instead of his son.

There is no way I could imagine what all was going on in Abraham's mind at these moments. God had promised Abraham a son at an old age beyond child bearing age, and here He wants this only son given as a sacrifice. The instructions were to build an altar at the top of the mountain and place this son on the alter. Abraham was fully obedient, and God provided Abraham and his son with lamb chops for dinner that night. What an awesome God we serve and how He rewards us in such unusual ways for our obedience.

Next in Deut.1: 36, "Caleb the son of Jephunneh; he shall see it, and to him and his children I am giving the land on which he walked, because he wholly followed the Lord." Caleb returned with a true report after spying the land that pleased God. As simple and small a task as that was, it shows how God is interested in the details no matter how big or small. Our obedience is what pleases Him. Because of Caleb's returning with a report that was in line with God's plan, Caleb became the first homesteader. Regardless of what God is calling us to do, we must remember that He always prepares and equips us for the task.

Another is in Josh. 6: 20 as Joshua is leading the people of Israel. "So the people shouted when the priests blew the trumpets. And it happened when the people heard the sound of the trumpet, and the people shouted with a great shout, that the wall fell down flat. Then the people went up into the city, every man straight before him, and they took the city." Sometimes God's plan does not make sense to us as in this time here. God's instruction was for the people to march around the city once a day for six days and then on the seventh day we pick up here in this passage. As I thought on this passage, I thought of two different views: One is the children of Israel looking at the city of Jericho from the outside and then the people inside watching what was going on each day as this group of people marched around their city. I am sure the children of Israel were wondering what is this going to accomplish as they marched around the city each day. The people on the inside were probably laughing about what was going on outside. A lessen for us here is doing things God's way is always the right way regardless of what makes sense to us. Sometimes God calls us to do some strange things. What the world will think is stupid, and yet we must not trust popular opinions, but the Lord.

In Dan. 3: 24-27 we see how three men refuse to be like everyone else and stand for the Lord. They refused to worship the golden image. "Look!" he answered, "I see four men loose, walking in the midst of the fire; and they are not hurt, and the form of the fourth is like the Son of God." 26Then Nebuchadnezzar went near the mouth of the burning fiery furnace and spoke, saying, "Shadrach, Meshach, and Abed-Nego, servants of the Most High God, come out, and come here." Then Shadrach, Meshach, and Abed-Nego came from the midst of the fire. 27And the satraps, administrators, governors, and the king's counselors gathered together, and they saw these men on whose bodies the fire had no power; the hair of their head was not singed nor were their garments affected, and the smell of fire was not on them.

I am reminded in 1 Kings 18 about the account of Elijah standing against the 400 prophets of Baal. In both cases we see how the Lord provides and protects those who stand up for the Lord. I remember being in a large meeting some years ago where many well known pastors and denominational leaders were present. During the discussion was a strategy presented that was contrary to the Bible. After hearing all of their presentation, I spoke up about following the Biblical pattern and was told that does not work anymore. My response was that it did not work if you did not do it. Their response to me was cutting me off. Not one person there supported me and is a matter of fact some criticized me for my stand. Some time later, one by one some apologized for not standing with me. They admitted I was right, and they were wrong. It has proved out over time that I was spot on. Since then many have more respect for me, and have a greater respect for my stand on God's word. It is not easy standing against the multitude, but it is worth standing for God's Word every time and for God's work to be fruitful regardless if no one stands with us.

Dan. 6: 21-22 gives us an example of praying to the Creator God rather than to the king. Then Daniel said to the king, "O king, live forever! 22My God sent His angel and shut the lions' mouths, so that they have not hurt me, because I was found innocent before Him; and also,

O king, I have done no wrong before you." A law was passed in that day that all prayers were to be to the king. Daniel refused to follow the law which violated God's Word and was placed in a lion's den full of hungry lions. Because of Daniel's desire to be faithful to the Lord and being placed in such danger, the Lord not only protected him, but used that set of circumstances to bring people to honor the Creator God. We may be called upon sometime to make a stand. As we face challenges, we may stand alone, but God is with us and will confirm to us we are in His will and His ways. The main thing is to be sure we are following His will. What will be your response?

You may have examples in your own life of disobedience and the consequences you endured as a result of some bad decision. You may have examples in your own life of obedience to God and how He rewarded you.

1. *Obedience matters for our daily joy* Acts 2:28 "You have made known to me the ways of life; You will make me full of joy in Your presence."

2. *Obedience matters for our rewards in Heaven* Matt. 16:27 "For the Son of Man will come in the glory of His Father with His angels, and then He will reward each according to his works."

3. *Obedience matters for our Salvation* John 14:6 Jesus said to him, "I am the way, the truth, and the life. No one comes to the Father except through Me." Choosing to follow our Lord is the greatest decision in life.

Josh. 3:17 "Then the priests who bore the ark of the covenant of the Lord stood firm on dry ground in the midst of the Jordan; and all Israel crossed over on dry ground, until all the people had crossed completely over the Jordan." Victory comes as we follow God's plans and do things God's way.

As you have seen from Scripture shared of God's faithfulness to His commands, how does your life stand before God? What is God's plan for you and me?

Please read Eph. 2: 1-10

CHAPTER 4

Joshua 4:
Crossing Jordan

And it came to pass, when all the people had completely crossed over the Jordan, that the Lord spoke to Joshua, saying: 2"Take for yourselves twelve men from the people, one man from every tribe, 3 and command them, saying, 'Take for yourselves twelve stones from here, out of the midst of the Jordan, from the place where the priests' feet stood firm. You shall carry them over with you and leave them in the lodging place where you lodge tonight.' " 4 Then Joshua called the twelve men whom he had appointed from the children of Israel, one man from every tribe; 5 and Joshua said to them: "Cross over before the ark of the Lord your God into the midst of the Jordan, and each one of you take up a stone on his shoulder, according to the number of the tribes of the children of Israel, 6 that this may be a sign among you when your children ask in time to come, saying, 'What do these stones mean to you?' 7 Then you shall answer them that the waters of the Jordan were cut off before the ark of the covenant of the Lord; when it crossed over the Jordan, the waters of the Jordan were cut off. And these stones shall be for a memorial to the children of Israel forever." 18 And it came to pass, when the priests who bore the ark of the covenant of the Lord had come from the midst of the Jordan, and the soles of the priests' feet touched the dry land, that the waters of the Jordan returned to their place and overflowed all its banks as before. 19 Now the people came up from the Jordan on the tenth day of the first month, and they camped in Gilgal on the east border of Jericho. 20 And those twelve stones which they took out of the Jordan, Joshua set up in Gilgal. 21 Then he spoke to the children of Israel, saying: "When your children ask their fathers in time to come, saying, 'What are these stones?' 22 then you shall let your children know, saying, 'Israel crossed over this Jordan on dry land'; 23 for the Lord your God dried up the waters of the Jordan before you until you had crossed over, as the Lord your God did to the Red Sea, which He dried up before us until we had crossed over, 24 that all the peoples of the earth may know the hand of the Lord, that it is mighty, that you may fear the Lord your God forever."

The children of Israel had just experienced a miracle of God by crossing the Jordan River at flood stage on dry ground. God demonstrated His power to them by stopping the flow of water in the river, and they were able to enter the Promise Land as He had promised their forefathers many years before. They were instructed by God to set up a memorial by gathering stones and placing them near the edge of the river to be a reminder of God's faithfulness to His people. They did that in Gilgal. God wanted this to be a testimony to the generations following to know of His commitment to His people. In verses 21-24, we see how God did not want them to forget, nor the generations to come to be unaware of His desire for His people to honor Him.

How soon we have a tendency to forget all of the blessings when things are going great in our lives. These people had come to what I call a crossroad decision or obey God's instruction. Looking at their situation seemed impossible. All things are possible with God according to His will. They chose to follow God's plan and experienced God's faithfulness to care for His people. If we want what is best for us, we need to follow God's plan for our daily lives. That is starting each day in His Word and in prayer seeking His direction. Included in my morning prayer is the desire to be sensitive to His Holy Spirit and for our Lord to provide opportunities to be a witness For Him. The more we see Him working in and through our lives, the more exciting life is. Excitement is contagious, and we need to be sharing how Our Lord is providing opportunities for us to share with others by lifting up His Name.

CHAPTER 5

Obedience Leads To Praise

And it came to pass, when all the kings of the Amorites, which were on the side of Jordan westward, and all the kings of the Canaanites, which were by the sea, heard that the LORD had dried up the waters of Jordan from before the children of Israel, until we were passed over, that their heart melted, neither was there spirit in them any more, because of the children of Israel. (5:1)

Their enemies had seen the awesome power of Almighty God and how He had provided for His people. As God provides for us, the people of the world are taking note of how God provides for us as His people. They may not understand how God is providing for His people, but they are watching.

In verses 2-8, the Lord reminds Joshua of the importance of the right fellowship with our Savior. He reminds them of the instruction God had given many years before and how that had been neglected. As we look in this section of Scripture, we are reminded of the importance to live in obedience to all of God's word.

9 And the LORD said unto Joshua, This day have I rolled away the reproach of Egypt from off you. Wherefore the name of the place is called Gilgal unto this day.

Joshua under God's directions gives the children of Israel a lesson in basic history. He reflects back on the their previous generation's journey from bondage in Egypt and through the wilderness. All of the ups and downs of the trip were worthy of notice. Here we see a generation lost due to disobedience and lack of appreciation for a Holy God The opportunity for a second chance was given here for this group of people. I am so glad that we are given the opportunity for a second chance, a third chance and many more as well. 1 John 1:9 "If we confess our sins, He is faithful and just to forgive us our sins and cleanse us from all unrighteousness," is a verse that should be near our hearts as we journey through the ups and downs in life to ensure we maintain the right fellowship with our Lord. Having that right fellowship with our Lord daily enables us to face each day with a right attitude toward every life situation.

In verse 9, we see the reward of following God's instruction. As we read through the word of God, we see a number of examples of seeing people following God's instructions and the rewards for doing so. The same applies for us today. As we follow our Lord's direction, we experience His blessings on our lives.

In verses 10-12, we see an interesting set of cause and effects.

10 And the children of Israel encamped in Gilgal, and kept the passover on the fourteenth day of the month at even in the plains of Jericho. 11 And they did eat of the old corn of the land on the morrow after the passover, unleavened cakes, and parched corn in the selfsame day. 12 And the manna ceased on the morrow after they had eaten of the old corn of the land; neither had the children of Israel manna any more; but they did eat of the fruit of the land of Canaan that year. God had been providing manna each day for their food. Now there was plenty of food in this new land for them to eat. 13 And it came to pass, when Joshua was by Jericho, that he lifted up his eyes and looked, and, behold, there stood a man over against him with his sword drawn in his hand: and Joshua went unto him, and said unto him, Art thou for us, or for our adversaries? 14 And he said, Nay; but as captain of the host of the LORD am I now come. And Joshua fell on his face to the earth, and did worship, and said unto him, What saith my lord unto his servant? 15 And the captain of the LORD'S host said unto Joshua, Loose thy shoe from off thy foot; for the place whereon thou standest is Holy. And Joshua did so.

There is a beautiful song, "Standing on Holy Ground," that is one of my favorites. It reminds me of God's presence. No matter what we are going through in life, He is always with us.

Mary and I were away from home thousands of miles away for a Christian meeting. We were awakened by shuffling feet early one morning moving on the ground to pray. It is so encouraging to realize that no matter wherever we find ourselves we have holy ground.

Because the children of Israel listened and obeyed the Lord, they were able to see God's blessing upon their lives. As they drew closer to the Lord, they saw the need to celebrate what He was doing in their lives. They were praising the Lord for His provisions and realized just how wonderful it was to be forgiven. Also, they realized in the closeness to the Lord that even the ground they were standing on was Holy. Wherever we find ourselves is Holy ground. God can use us in unusual and unexpected places. How humbling it was to know these people were going there to pray for us as we were going to share with them that morning! God blessed their faithfulness to prayer and personal sacrifice for this meeting.

The farther we get from the Lord, the more a sin nature becomes more inviting. Our joy begins to fade away and our desire to be around other believers vanishes, as well as our desire to read His Word.. The closer we come to the Lord, the greater the desire to honor Him with our lives. We sense the presence of the Holy Spirit and see the need to draw even closer to the Lord. As a result, we find ourselves feasting on His Word and on our faces before Him.

CHAPTER 6

Victory In The Morning

This entire chapter demonstrates how God gives us victory as we fully obey Him even when His plans seem illogical to us. Sometimes we feel like we have a better idea, or we want to add to His plan, or even take away from His plan.

6:1 Now Jericho was straitly shut up because of the children of Israel: none went out, and none came in. 2 And the LORD said unto Joshua, See, I have given into thine hand Jericho, and the king thereof, and the mighty men of valour. 3 And ye shall compass the city, all ye men of war, and go round about the city once. Thus shalt thou do six days. 4 And seven priests shall bear before the ark seven trumpets of rams' horns: and the seventh day ye shall compass the city seven times, and the priests shall blow with the trumpets. 5 And it shall come to pass, that when they make a long blast with the ram's horn, and when ye hear the sound of the trumpet, all the people shall shout with a great shout; and the wall of the city shall fall down flat, and the people shall ascend up every man straight before him.6 And Joshua the son of Nun called the priests, and said unto them, Take up the ark of the covenant, and let seven priests bear seven trumpets of rams' horns before the ark of the LORD.

7 And he said unto the people, Pass on, and compass the city, and let him that is armed pass on before the ark of the LORD. 8 And it came to pass, when Joshua had spoken unto the people, that the seven priests bearing the seven trumpets of rams' horns passed on before the LORD, and blew with the trumpets: and the ark of the covenant of the LORD followed them. 9 And the armed men went before the priests that blew with the trumpets, and the rear guard came after the ark, the priests going on, and blowing with the trumpets.10 And Joshua had commanded the people, saying, Ye shall not shout, nor make any noise with your voice, neither shall any word proceed out of your mouth, until the day I bid you shout; then shall ye shout. 11 So the ark of the LORD compassed the city, going about it once: and they came into the camp, and lodged in the camp. 12 And Joshua rose early in the morning, and the priests took up the ark of the LORD.

13 And seven priests bearing seven trumpets of rams' horns before the ark of the LORD went on continually, and blew with the trumpets: and the armed men went before them; but the rear guard came after the ark of the LORD, the priests going on, and blowing with the trumpets. 14 And the second day they compassed the city once, and returned into the camp: so they did six days.15 And it came to pass on the seventh day, that they

rose early about the dawning of the day, and compassed the city after the same manner seven times: only on that day they compassed the city seven times.

16 And it came to pass at the seventh time, when the priests blew with the trumpets, Joshua said unto the people, Shout; for the LORD hath given you the city.

Sometimes we question God's directions. I am certain the people of Jericho were wondering what the people of God were doing each day as they marched around their city. Just as they had questions, I can not help thinking there were questions for some of those marching around the city. All of their questions were answered on that seventh day as the children of God shouted and the walls fell to the ground. There are times God calls on us to do things that seem strange to us. Many times we feel we are not prepared nor equipped for the task the Lord has for us. We must remember to trust Him in every task He leads us to do.

17 And the city shall be accursed, even it, and all that are therein, to the LORD: only Rahab the harlot shall live, she and all that are with her in the house, because she hid the messengers that we sent. 18 And ye, in any wise keep yourselves from the accursed thing, lest ye make yourselves accursed, when ye take of the accursed thing, and make the camp of Israel a curse, and trouble it. 19 But all the silver, and gold, and vessels of brass and iron, are consecrated unto the LORD: they shall come into the treasury of the LORD. 20 So the people shouted when the priests blew with the trumpets: and it came to pass, when the people heard the sound of the trumpet,

and the people shouted with a great shout, that the wall fell down flat, so that the people went up into the city, every man straight before him, and they took the city. 21 And they utterly destroyed all that was in the city, both man and woman, young and old, and ox, and sheep, and ass, with the edge of the sword. 22 But Joshua had said unto the two men that had spied out the country, Go into the harlot's house, and bring out thence the woman, and all that she hath, as ye sware unto her. 23 And the young men that were spies went in, and brought out Rahab, and her father, and her mother, and her brethren, and all that she had; and they brought out all her kindred, and left them without the camp of Israel. 24 And they burnt the city with fire, and all that was therein: only the silver, and the gold, and the vessels of brass and of iron, they put into the treasury of the house of the LORD. 25 And Joshua saved Rahab the harlot alive, and her father's household, and all that she had; and she dwelleth in Israel even unto this day; because she hid the messengers, which Joshua sent to spy out Jericho. 26 And Joshua adjured them at that time, saying, Cursed be the man before the LORD, that riseth up and buildeth this city Jericho: he shall lay the foundation thereof in his firstborn, and in his youngest son shall he set up the gates of it. 27 So the LORD was with Joshua; and his fame was noised throughout all the country.

The people here witnessed God's mighty power. He had provided victory over the mighty men of war in Jericho. Sometimes we are faced with our own battles in life that seem so overwhelming, yet our Lord is able to give us the victory as we allow Him to fight our battles in life. He works in ways that may seem strange to us.

I had a lady in one of the churches I was blessed to serve in as pastor who had a daughter who was living a horrible lifestyle. The mother came to me requesting prayer for her daughter. We prayed and I asked God to do whatever it took to stop this young lady from her current lifestyle and turn her life to the Lord. The next day she was arrested and put in jail. Her mom went down and got her out of jail a couple of days later. A few weeks passed, and the young lady was doing even worse than before. Here comes her mom back to my office desiring for me to pray for her again. I told the mom that we had prayed before, and she had decided to help God by getting her out of jail. I told the mom I would pray again with her, but please give time to see it through God's way.

A few days later this daughter was put in jail and spent a year in jail. Just before getting out, this daughter called me wanting an appointment with me to talk about her commitment to the Lord. She got out of jail and was faithful in coming to church (while I was there). This mom experienced God's victory by letting God work according to His plan. We can see victory in our own lives as we pray, follow His will daily, and trusting Him with all the details as we watch His faithfulness to us. You may have a friend, relative, or neighbor you have been praying for. Do not give up!

CHAPTER 7

THE AGONY OF DEFEAT

Sin has consequences, and here is a good example. Achan's sin affected him, his family, others and all that he had. God gave him every chance to repent, but he chose not to humble himself before a Holy God.

Many times our defeats are self imposed by our own actions because we feel that what we do does not affect anyone else. We have the opportunity to confess when we have sinned and know that we have 1 John 1:9 to restore our right fellowship with our Lord. Maintaining a right fellowship is key to having the abundant life filled with the joy of the Lord.

7:1 But the children of Israel committed a trespass in the accursed thing: for Achan, the son of Carmi, the son of Zabdi, the son of Zerah, of the tribe of Judah, took of the accursed thing: and the anger of the LORD was kindled against the children of Israel.

Disobedience causes our fellowship with our Lord to be broken. When fellowship is broken by disobedience, we must practice 1 John 1:9 to restore our fellowship with our Lord. Achan refused to admit his sin and tried to cover it up. The Lord sees everything we do and takes note. Achan was not able to hide from God and neither are we able able to hide from our Lord. (*Note*: in the following passage, the comments in parentheses are mine.)

2 And Joshua sent men from Jericho to Ai, which is beside Bethaven, on the east side of Bethel, and spake unto them, saying, Go up and view the country. And the men went up and viewed Ai. (Sin always gives a distorted view of the truth). 4 So there went up thither of the people about three thousand men: and they fled before the men of Ai. (Sin here caused them to be defeated in what should have been a simple task. From this we can see how sin does have consequences.) 5 And the men of Ai smote of them about thirty and six men: for they chased them from before the gate even unto Shebarim, and smote them in the going down: wherefore the hearts of the people melted, and became as water. (The sin of one man caused many to be affected by his ungodliness.) 6 And Joshua rent his clothes, and fell to the earth upon his face before the ark of the LORD until the eventide, he and the elders of Israel, and put dust upon their heads.

7 And Joshua said, Alas, O Lord GOD, wherefore hast thou at all brought this people over Jordan, to deliver us into the hand of the Amorites, to destroy us? would to God we had been content, and dwelt on the other side Jordan! 8 O Lord, what shall I say, when Israel turneth their backs before their enemies! 9 For the Canaanites and all the inhabitants of the land shall hear

of it, and shall environ us round, and cut off our name from the earth: and what wilt thou do unto thy great name? 10 And the LORD said unto Joshua, Get thee up; wherefore liest thou thus upon thy face? 11 Israel hath sinned, and they have also transgressed my covenant which I commanded them: for they have even taken of the accursed thing, and have also stolen, and dissembled also, and they have put it even among their own stuff. (Wrongful behavior cannot be hidden from God.) 12 Therefore the children of Israel could not stand before their enemies, but turned their backs before their enemies, because they were accursed: neither will I be with you any more, except ye destroy the accursed from among you. (This shows how much God dislikes sin. He will not tolerate disobedience. The Holy Spirit convicts us and He demands our response.) 13 Get up, sanctify the people, and say, Sanctify yourselves against tomorrow: for thus saith the LORD God of Israel, There is an accursed thing in the midst of thee, O Israel: thou canst not stand before thine enemies, until ye take away the accursed thing from among you. (Sin must be handled.) 14 In the morning therefore ye shall be brought according to your tribes: and it shall be, that the tribe which the LORD taketh shall come according to the families thereof; and the family which the LORD shall take shall come by households; and the household which the LORD shall take shall come man by man. 15 And it shall be, that he that is taken with the accursed thing shall be burnt with fire, he and all that he hath: because he hath transgressed the covenant of the LORD, and because he hath wrought folly in Israel. 16 So Joshua rose up early in the morning, and brought Israel by their tribes; and the tribe of Judah was taken:

17 And he brought the family of Judah; and he took the family of the Zarhites: and he brought the family of the Zarhites man by man; and Zabdi was taken: 18 And he brought his household man by man; and Achan, the son of Carmi, the son of Zabdi, the son of Zerah, of the tribe of Judah, was taken. 19 And Joshua said unto Achan, My son, give, I pray thee, glory to the LORD God of Israel, and make confession unto him; and tell me now what thou hast done; hide it not from me. 20 And Achan answered Joshua, and said, Indeed I have sinned against the LORD God of Israel, and thus and thus have I done: 21 When I saw among the spoils a goodly Babylonish garment, and two hundred shekels of silver, and a wedge of gold of fifty shekels weight, then I coveted them, and took them; and, behold, they are hid in the earth in the midst of my tent, and the silver under it. 22 So Joshua sent messengers, and they ran unto the tent; and, behold, it was hid in his tent, and the silver under it. 23 And they took them out of the midst of the tent, and brought them unto Joshua, and unto all the children of Israel, and laid them out before the LORD. 24 And Joshua, and all Israel with him, took Achan the son of Zerah, and the silver, and the garment, and the wedge of gold, and his sons, and his daughters, and his oxen, and his asses, and his sheep, and his tent, and all that he had: and they brought them unto the valley of Achor. 25 And Joshua said, Why hast thou troubled us? the LORD

shall trouble thee this day. And all Israel stoned him with stones, and burned them with fire, after they had stoned them with stones. 26 And they raised over him a great heap of stones unto this day. So the LORD turned from the fierceness of his anger. Wherefore the name of that place was called, The valley of Achor, unto this day.

It is so sad that all this tragedy took place because of one man's greed. So many lives were lost and families hurt by Achan's covetousness. That kind of thing happens too often today in our world. We need to be thankful for what God has blessed us with. He has promised to supply all of our needs, and we must remember that does not include our "want list". Our loving Heavenly Father knows more of what we need than we do. I am so thankful for His provisions. He has always provided and right on time.

I am reminded of a man of much wealth who was constantly trying to have more and more. He was never satisfied with what he had accumulated. In his search for more and more, he turned his family and friends away. He died alone and wanting no one to visit him in his last moments of life. His life had been consumed by greed and after his death, there was no memorial service. By the time of his death, he had lost all that he had accumulated. His lifestyle was a sad testimony to his family. They were embarrassed to admit their relationship to him. He lived by the saying that what he did was his business and no one else's business. He believed that what he did did not impact anyone else. How wrong he was.

We must be satisfied with what we have and be thankful. Mary and I learned a valuable lesson about this as we traveled to a foreign country. We saw many that had very little and yet had joy because of their relationship with the Lord. We both realized that we had been blessed with a lot of stuff. We are thankful for what we have and have given much away to those in need. As we have given to others, God has blessed us with more to share with others.

CHAPTER 8

Moving Ahead

Sitting around having a pity party because things did not go our way never accomplishes anything. Sometimes when bad things happen, people are quick to say, "Why did God allow this to happen to me?" Instead of looking at the obstacles or disappointments of bad and unexpected things that happen, why not seek God's directions and look at this as an opportunity to grow in Him? God knows when we hurt, and we do when the unexpected happens, but He has given us the Comforter to help us in our grief times. What I am saying is we do have to go through the grief process when we have bad things, but God is able to give us directions and comfort, especially through the love and support of others in our lives.

Defeats have a tendency to discourage us at times, yet in this case there was a need to deal with an internal problem. This problem was exposed and God had given instructions on how to deal with the problem. He continues to do this for us today through His Word. In 1 & 2 Corinthians, Paul gives us examples of problems and how to address them. He knows we have situations arise in our daily lives where Satan attempts to draw us off course. Satan is our enemy and works hard to distract us from staying on course with our Lord. There was sin in the camp, and it had to be dealt with. After the sin problem was taken care of, they were ready to move ahead and experience the blessings of the Lord.

8:1 And the LORD said unto Joshua, Fear not, neither be thou dismayed: take all the people of war with thee, and arise, go up to Ai: see, I have given into thy hand the king of Ai, and his people, and his city, and his land: 2 And thou shalt do to Ai and her king as thou didst unto Jericho and her king: only the spoil thereof, and the cattle thereof, shall ye take for a prey unto yourselves: lay thee an ambush for the city behind it. When we have bad or unexpected events in life, we must not allow them to stop us. It is most important that we move ahead to accomplish the plans of our Lord.

Here God tells them it is time to get up and go. We can not live on past victories nor failures. It is impossible for us to turn back the hands of time. We must look ahead to accomplish the work God has for us.

18 And the LORD said unto Joshua, Stretch out the spear that is in thy hand toward Ai; for I will give it into thine hand. And Joshua stretched out the spear that he had in his hand toward the city.

This verse has such encouragement. They knew now the victory at Ai was a God thing. The battle here, as in

Jericho, was the Lord's battle and this prepared them for the task ahead in conquering the cities ahead.

After reading this passage, I am reminded of a light shower of rain in the summer that brings a coolness to break the heat as well as refreshing aroma to the air. Those people had just gone through a difficult time in life, and God brings a refreshing new look for them as He demonstrates His faithfulness and love for them through this victory at Ai. Certainly this had to be an encouraging moment for the children of God to see His mighty power at work. A time to build their faith in the One Who was providing and guiding them day by day. Just as The Lord worked for them, He does the same for us as we follow His guidance in our lives. As we obediently follow His will in our lives, we experience the joy He has for each of us daily.

Many times throughout Scripture we see the word "remember" as God points to different events where He demonstrated His provisions and wanted the evidence of the event as a testimony to the following generations. He has given us His Holy Word for us to see these mighty acts as a reminder for us today of His faithfulness and love. His word is also a reminder of those who rebelled against God and the consequences that followed as a warning to us to keep our focus on our Savior.

CHAPTER 9

Joshua 9-12:

Conquering The Promise Land

These four chapters cover the many battles the children of Israel faced each day as they marched ahead in obedience to God to conquer the promise land. They experienced many ups and downs during this part of their journey. This reminds me of our daily journey in life. It is filled with many ups and downs like a roller coaster. Just as these people saw God at work in their daily battles, we see God at work in our lives as we deal with life situations each and everyday. I cannot help but wonder how many times God has provided or protected us when we did not even know He was watching over us.

In this next section of verses, we see an account of a group of people claiming one thing, and it is later found out the untruths told in order to cover their real reasons for asking for help. We must be careful about everyone coming to us for any reason. So many times they have false motives as did this group of people. It is important for us to pray seeking God's will and His discernment. The children of God neglected to pray first which was a mistake. We need to pray first about every decision to avoid the mistake presented here.

9:1 And it came to pass, when all the kings who were on this side of the Jordan, in the hills and in the lowland and in all the coasts of the Great Sea toward Lebanon—the Hittite, the Amorite, the Canaanite, the Perizzite, the Hivite, and the Jebusite—heard about it, 2 that they gathered together to fight with Joshua and Israel with one accord. 3 But when the inhabitants of Gibeon heard what Joshua had done to Jericho and Ai, 4 they worked craftily, and went and pretended to be ambassadors. And they took old sacks on their donkeys, old wineskins torn and mended, 5 old and patched sandals on their feet, and old garments on themselves; and all the bread of their provision was dry and moldy. 6 And they went to Joshua, to the camp at Gilgal, and said to him and to the men of Israel, "We have come from a far country; now therefore, make a covenant with us." 7 Then the men of Israel said to the Hivites, "Perhaps you dwell among us; so how can we make a covenant with you?" 8 But they said to Joshua, "We are your servants." And Joshua said to them, "Who are you, and where do you come from?" 9 So they said to him: "From a very far country your servants have come, because of the name of the Lord your God; for we have heard of His fame, and all that He did in Egypt, 10 and all that He did to the two kings of the

Amorites who were beyond the Jordan—to Sihon king of Heshbon, and Og king of Bashan, who was at Ashtaroth. 11 Therefore our elders and all the inhabitants of our country spoke to us, saying, 'Take provisions with you for the journey, and go to meet them, and say to them, "We are your servants; now therefore, make a covenant with us." '12 This bread of ours we took hot for our provision from our houses on the day we departed to come to you. But now look, it is dry and moldy. 13 And these wineskins which we filled were new, and see, they are torn; and these our garments and our sandals have become old because of the very long journey." 14 Then the men of Israel took some of their provisions; but they did not ask counsel of the Lord. 15 So Joshua made peace with them, and made a covenant with them to let them live; and the rulers of the congregation swore to them. 16 And it happened at the end of three days, after they had made a covenant with them, that they heard that they were their neighbors who dwelt near them.

Sadly not everyone is truthful. This group had been untruthful to the children of God and because of their commitment ended up being an added burden. I had a person come to my office sharing a need for medication for his supposed medical condition. During our conversation, I felt that something was wrong, and soon found out he had been hitting churches from Jacksonville, Florida to Gulf Port, Mississippi. After calling a local drug store who had already gotten an alert about this guy, I found that my uncertainty was right on the mark. I was kind and loving to this guy, but sent him on his way.

17 Then the children of Israel journeyed and came to their cities on the third day. Now their cities were Gibeon, Chephirah, Beeroth, and Kirjath Jearim. 18 But the children of Israel did not attack them, because the rulers of the congregation had sworn to them by the Lord God of Israel. And all the congregation complained against the rulers. 19 Then all the rulers said to all the congregation, "We have sworn to them by the Lord God of Israel; now therefore, we may not touch them. 20 This we will do to them: We will let them live, lest wrath be upon us because of the oath which we swore to them." 21 And the rulers said to them, "Let them live, but let them be woodcutters and water carriers for all the congregation, as the rulers had promised them." 22 Then Joshua called for them, and he spoke to them, saying, "Why have you deceived us, saying, 'We are very far from you,' when you dwell near us? 23 Now therefore, you are cursed, and none of you shall be freed from being slaves—woodcutters and water carriers for the house of my God." 24 So they answered Joshua and said, "Because your servants were clearly told that the Lord your God commanded His servant Moses to give you all the land, and to destroy all the inhabitants of the land from before you; therefore we were very much afraid for our lives because of you, and have done this thing. 25 And now, here we are, in your hands; do with us as it seems good and right to do to us." 26 So he did to them, and delivered them out of the hand of the children of Israel, so that they did not kill them. 27 And that day Joshua made them woodcutters and water carriers for the congrega-

tion and for the altar of the Lord, in the place which He would choose, even to this day.

Although they were given slave type jobs, this group of people limited the children of God's ability to effectively accomplish what God had for them. Sometimes Satan will put an opportunity in our path that seems right, but takes our focus off of the task our Lord has for us. We must be on the alert about everything. Satan is constantly looking for ways to distract us from obeying God. We must allow God's discernment to guide us at all times.

10:1 Now it came to pass when Adoni-Zedek king of Jerusalem heard how Joshua had taken Ai and had utterly destroyed it—as he had done to Jericho and its king, so he had done to Ai and its king—and how the inhabitants of Gibeon had made peace with Israel and were among them, 2 that they feared greatly, because Gibeon was a great city, like one of the royal cities, and because it was greater than Ai, and all its men were mighty. 3 Therefore Adoni-Zedek king of Jerusalem sent to Hoham king of Hebron, Piram king of Jarmuth, Japhia king of Lachish, and Debir king of Eglon, saying, 4 "Come up to me and help me, that we may attack Gibeon, for it has made peace with Joshua and with the children of Israel." 5 Therefore the five kings of the Amorites, the king of Jerusalem, the king of Hebron, the king of Jarmuth, the king of Lachish, and the king of Eglon, gathered together and went up, they and all their armies, and camped before Gibeon and made war against it.

These five kings were trusting in their own combined power. They had witnessed the mighty hand of God battling the enemies of Israel and for some reason did not consider Who they were waring against. All five of these kings and their armies were destroyed by a faithful God. Fighting against Almighty God is always a bad decision. As we have daily battles in our daily journey in life, we should aways allow God to battle for us. As a result we see continued victories and experience God's faithfulness.

The closing words in chapter twelve tells us that thirty-one kings were defeated. If we look at this entire section of all of these battles one after another that these people faced day after day, it would be overwhelming. I am so glad that God does not show us large blocks of time of future situations causing us to be overwhelmed, too. We only see through what I call a soda straw, and God sees the big picture.

Just as God called Abraham to leave the land of Ur to go to a land that He would show them and He guided them day by day, these people understood God's command for them to conquer the land God had promised them. They were looking ahead and focused on the promise of God. As they saw first hand how God won their daily battles, it certainly was a faith builder for them and to see God's faithfulness. I think of the old hymn entitled "Count Your Blessings." If we begin to acknowledge all our Lord is doing for each of us each and everyday, our hearts should be overflowing with praise and joy. It is difficult when going through hard times. I know first hand as I have been in this journey with cancer.

It began with a wrong diagnosis that continued for fourteen months with getting sicker each day and losing seventy-five pounds. I had to eventually retire in March of 2022 after pastoring and ministry positions for 40 years. A determined nurse practitioner would not stop until he found my problem of kidney cancer. Treatment began soon afterwards only to be ineffective in removing the cancer completely. God has been in the midst of this journey providing opportunities to share with people in the hospital during each of my stays. Additionally, after I had to retire, Mary and I joined Cottage Hill Baptist Church here in Mobile, AL. There I was asked to be a teacher of adults and got to teach three different times as I have been able. Also I got to speak in a local church for the emphasis on international missions on the first Sunday in December.

In January, 2023, I began working with medical personnel at M D Anderson, Houston, TX. While here at this hospital now for the strenuous treatment prescribed to rid me of cancer, I am proof reading this manuscript for the publisher for final changes on March 28, 2023. I am praying, as so many others are, that this treatment will remove the lymphoma and leukemia permanently that I have. I will be going to this hospital for periodic checkups, but Mary and I have been encouraged by the information and responses of pre- CAR T steps of the CAR T treatment plan which will be on Friday, March 31. I have been getting stronger and have improved in many ways already from previous treatment that did not remove it. We are believing God again for another miracle in our lives. As you read this, you can offer prayers, too, that we definitely do appreciate.

I am not at the end of the journey, but I am encouraged knowing God is with me and is faithful. As I write, I am seeking to fulfill His calling on my life to share Jesus through writing. Even though I cannot travel for now, I am praying that God will use this book to encourage others to continue to be faithful regardless of the circumstances. He has promised to be with us and to never forsake us. This promise always brings comfort and is for each and every one of us as we face our own daily battles. We must remind ourselves that our Lord is with us every step of the way. I am not sure how many of you are familiar with the poem "Footprints," but look it up. It is a beautiful reminder of God's presence even when we are unsure of His plans forward, but we have the assurance of His presence in our daily lives.

CHAPTER 10

Joshua 13-22

Dividing the Land

13:1 Now Joshua was old, advanced in years. And the Lord said to him: "You are old, advanced in years, and there remains very much land yet to be possessed. 2 This is the land that yet remains: all the territory of the Philistines and all that of the Geshurites, 3 from Sihor, which is east of Egypt, as far as the border of Ekron northward (which is counted as Canaanite); the five lords of the Philistines--the Gazites, the Ashdodites, the Ashkelonites, the Gittites, and the Ekronites; also the Avites; 4 from the south, all the land of the Canaanites, and Mearah that belongs to the Sidonians as far as Aphek, to the border of the Amorites; 5 the land of the Gebalites, and all Lebanon, toward the sunrise, from Baal Gad below Mount Hermon as far as the entrance to Hamath; 6 all the inhabitants of the mountains from Lebanon as far as the Brook Misrephoth, and all the Sidonians-

-them I will drive out from before the children of Israel; only divide it by lot to Israel as an inheritance, as I have commanded you. 7 Now therefore, divide this land as an inheritance to the nine tribes and half the tribe of Manasseh." 8 With the other half tribe the Reubenites and the Gadites received their inheritance, which Moses had given them, beyond the Jordan eastward, as Moses the servant of the Lord had given them:

God had given Moses instructions on how the land was to be divided between the tribes many years before. Joshua had the responsibility to complete the task of seeing the land was divided just as God had instructed so many years before. God fulfilled His covenant with His people and continues to do the same for us today. God's word is filled with His promises that ensure us of His commitment and faithfulness.

Over the years this has been a battleground for those opposed to God's people to maintain this land. People of the world have tried many times to eliminate God's people and His word unsuccessfully. War is going on in that area even to this very date.

CHAPTER 11

Joshua 23-24

Farewell

In chapter 23 we see God acknowledging the fact that Joshua is quite elderly as He calls for Joshua to speak to the leaders. In verses 3-5 Joshua is reminding them of what God had done in conquering the Promise Land. for them. In verse 6, God reminds them to keep what is written in the Law of Moses and turn aside to the right or to the left. The rest of the chapter deals with the consequences of not following God and being obedient to Him. God knew the ungodliness of these other nations, and He did not want the Israelites compromising their faith in Almighty God. The people had experienced the peace, joy and abundant life since conquering the Promise Land. He gave them this warning knowing the possibilities of the people.

It seems that when things are going well we begin looking at ourselves instead of looking upward. We must discipline ourselves to a commitment to God's word and fellowshipping with other believers.

The times we live in are such that lend themselves to get us distracted and out of touch in our Christian walk. The restrictions during Covid made it very difficult to attend church and fellowship with other believers.

However, this also provided a way get out of touch with our necessity for fellowshipping and encouraging one another. There is the reality that some have to work and take care of others during meeting times, but we still have to find ways to be together some way to fellowship and encourage one another. So many have become isolated during this time that has led to depression and discouragement, even to suicide. Man is made for connection, and as Christians, we are to be our brother's keeper and watch for these kinds of situations to let people know they are loved and to encourage them.

In chapter 24, Joshua goes through the history of how God had been with them from the flood, to Abraham, and then all the enemy nations to deliver them. He reminded them that he had brought them to a land where they had plenty.

Verse 15 is the very quoted verse he gave them that expresses his sincerity for his desire for them to fear the Lord and serve Him. 15 And if it seems evil to you to serve the Lord, choose for yourselves this day whom you will serve, whether the gods which your fathers served that were on the other side of the river or the gods of the Amorites, in whose land you dwell. But as for me and my house, we will serve the Lord.

Just as Joshua called out to the people to choose who

they would serve, we must do the same thing; whether the gods of this world or Jesus. The world is filled with all kinds of distractors, and anything that stands between us and God is a god. A number of times in Scripture we are told we cannot serve 2 masters. The very first of the commandments says we shall have no other gods before the Creator God. We cannot allow other things to stand between us and God. That is a choice we have to make. He is a jealous God, He has to be first place in every area of our lives. Serving Him brings the greatest joy, and we can only have that when He is first place.

In this passage the people answered that they would at which time Joshua told them to put away their false gods. He reminded them they could not serve God and the strange gods and that they would make a memorial stone at Shechem to remind them of their commitment.

Then Joshua died.

Today many people have a show of Christianity but down deep, there is not a real commitment. Each person has to look inside and see if they are truly saved and living a God honoring life to the best they can. The Bible teaches that we have to constantly hide God's word in our hearts so we will not sin against Him. (Ps. 119:11) The beautiful part is that when we do sin and we truly confess them repenting in sincerity, God will be faithful to forgive and remove those as far as the east is from the west. We then have the abundant life to live in submission to His will and plan for our lives.

What a joy to have this freedom in Christ! My prayer for each one reading this book is that you have found Jesus to be your strength and your song fully committed to Him serving Him in whatever place He has you serving for His honor and glory.

CHAPTER 12

Our Personal Experiences Of God's Faithfulness

Some of Our Missions Experiences

Laurel Lake Baptist Camp,
Corbin, KY, 1992

In June,1992, Mary and I had been on a trip to Corbin, KY. Mary had wanted a picture of a red barn. So we went searching for one in the rural areas when we spotted a sign that said Laurel Lake Baptist Campground. We drove into the area and found a picturesque area for a camp and a director who had just been there for a year. The young camp pastor and director, Patrick Callahan, had just arrived home from speaking at a church to get resources to renovate the camp formerly owned by Colonel Sanders. He was so overcome with grief at how to get this off the ground with no money or resources needed for repair. He was ready to resign that night. It definitely had many needs of repair. We talked and prayed with him a while and left with Mary crying over how could we be of help to restore this camp to its full use and capacities and bless this pastor/director.

We felt that God really wanted us to do that and began praying. We came back to Mobile and contacted Dr. Darrell Robinson, the former pastor of Dauphin Way Baptist church in Mobile and then the Evangelism Director for the North America Mission Board where he retired. Bro. Darrell was the pastor when I went to Dauphin Way and met Mary. We had him for our marriage counselor before the wedding.

We knew he had information as to how to do a missions endeavor. It was a short time later that we began getting letters from adults in different states ready to come help. By August a team had been formed and connected at the camp for a week of repairs. There were no funds to do the repairs or to provide food for the mission team. Patrick called me on Saturday morning before I left and said they had no money for materials. We had given him a list of the materials needed for the week we were there. Early on Monday morning, after arriving Sunday night, the materials were delivered and the ticket was paid for in full. God had provided that need. A group of ladies from one of the churches cooked the breakfast each day for us. We began working and the Manna House was in much worse shape than what was thought including a hidden hornet's nest that we were able to remove and not one person got stung. The terrain is mountainous, and the Manna House was situated on the edge of the mountain. The slant on the back was the highest point and looking down was a deep slope. You can imagine the tension associated with the replacement of the roof. On the front you could almost touch the ground .

As lunch time approached, we were wondering where to go for getting lunch when another group of ladies appeared with lunch. During the afternoon, Patrick received a call that a check for $5,000 had been given. That evening another church brought dinner, and this pattern continued the rest of the week. Then I began contacting the directors of missions for the 5 associations that owned the camp. A sixth one came on board while there. They had not been supporting it financially or being an encourager. Thursday I spoke to them, challenged them and prayed with them about how God could use that camp. For several years prior, they only used the camp only 3 to 4 weeks the entire year. On Wednesday night, each team member went to different churches to challenge them to help with the repairs for the camp.

Each night we had a devotion and prayed for God to meet the needs of that camp and use that camp. We completed the week on Friday evening and praised God for all He had done. As we were retuning home, Patrick called to tell us that there had been $25,000 raised for that camp. To this day the camp has been being used about 50 weeks of the year since we were there, and we still have close contact with Patrick who has raised eight children, and leadership for the camp during the summers. Now he has grandchildren to help.

Mary, Earnest, the youngest son, and I returned in August, 1993, to do repairs on some buildings and mowing the grass. Mary worked in the kitchen cooking and serving meals to many campers and volunteers. In the off times, she upgraded the missionary house where we were staying by doing some painting, purchasing needed supplies and some things to make it more beautiful. We helped her by cutting back a lot of the bushes and undergrowth around it. That trip was so special to her to get to see all the previous improvements and the prayers answered and efforts made before.

We praise God for getting our feet wet for missions here in the USA. We love camp ministry as well, and I am thankful I got to serve as interim Camp Director at Camp Whispering Pines in our Mobile Baptist Association for almost a year.

When I took the position, there was a new hotel in the progress of being built, due to the former building being destroyed by a hurricane. I had the opportunity to help with instruction on how to complete the process that became an attractive, useful housing location for camp participants. Other improvements have been completed, including a spacious multi-purpose activity building. This multi-acreage, beautiful camp, located in Citronelle, Alabama, continues to be used to reach, disciple, and encourage all who attend. Though dissters may come, we see God's faithfulness revealed to further promote His Kingdom work.

Mary and I have often used our home as a ministry center, especially for fellowship of large groups as well as Disciple Now Weekends for youth. We have enjoyed doing many conferences and retreats, often at campgrounds where we have seen God do such wonderful things in peoples' lives.

Our First Overseas Mission Trip to Wales, 1996

Our desires had been to serve God in church development which we had been doing. In 1995, I accepted the pastorate of a new church start getting my first opportunity of many that would follow to help in church planting and development.

Mary had retired as a high school counselor in the public schools of Mobile in 1995. In the spring of 1996, she was asked and accepted to be the third Director of the International Language School where she and I have served in the international missions area in Mobile Baptist Association for over 25 years now. In 2019, I retired in October as the International Ministries Director, having served 2 times prior as interim director when changes occurred. I did accept the pastorate of another small church, Smithtown Baptist, near our home, in 2018 and stayed there until the past year in March, 2022, when I knew that I was just not physically able to continue to do this ministry.

Dr. Cecil Taylor, a friend and former professor of mine at what is now University of Mobile, invited Mary and me to go with him to Wales in July of 1996 with some college students which was their first of many trips for the college to this area of the world. His wife, Rita, and Mary helped as well. We saw again how God will provide in financial ways as He has continued to do. We had six weeks to get the Passport for each and the funds raised for us to go. Another professor and his wife had had interferences that prevented their ability to go.

We had 14 people with students and the 2 other adults volunteering from elsewhere to go and help. We saw God work in miraculous ways as He opened doors for ministry and sharing of the gospel.

Two local pastors and wives helped the team and provided space for meetings in churches, all small and almost non-existent in that area of the world. Many large older ones were now museums. The churches provided homes for the team. We started on that first Saturday with a free BBQ on top of the mountain. The people did not know what to think. They stood at the bottom of the mountain trying to figure this out never seeing such a thing before.

That week we began doing outreach to reach children, and even older youth and young adults came to the holiday Bible club. We had to spread ourselves and do more groups than planned but had enough materials brought by plane to serve the Bible club. The church services were very special also. The seating was the old straight back board types that kept you alert. The ladies met for a Coffee Morning with devotions and fellowship each day.

We saw God save so many, especially 5 young 23 year-olds that did TV productions that I led to the Lord. They even taped some of the occasions to be shown on

TV. We realized mid-week that we needed to provide for some followup guidance for discipleship. God provided for growth of this group for a number of years. On the last Saturday there, we did another BBQ on the mountain at which time the people of the area came and helped us do the work, but they did not even want to eat just relishing these last moments to be with us. When we left on the bus, we were all crying as we watched the people lined up on the sides of the streets crying and begging us not to leave. We had our hearts so filled and wanted to stay.

In southern Wales, God gave us a passion for overseas missions that has followed us through the years in different locations.

International Missions in Mobile, 1996

As previously mentioned, Mary had retired from public school as a high school counselor. She was asked to take the position as Director of the International Language School for the Mobile Baptist Association, the ESL ministry for internationals in Mobile County in the spring before we left for Wales. In the late 70's, an influx of Vietnamese refugees came to Mobile which opened the door to enlarge the present ESL ministry in the churches to offer an associational approach but churches still hosted the classes. Mary was the third one as the leader, and during this time I worked with her. It was in early 1997 the opportunity came for me, and I was asked to serve as the Interim Vietnamese pastor for most of that year to the Vietnamese Baptist Mission hosted in one of the churches. We were SO blessed to see God save and minister to so many of this nationality that has remained close to us to this day.

God used this time for me to open my heart more for missions to internationals right here in Mobile which has continued. Mary and I have enjoyed this area for more than 25 years and hosted many young people in college and in working positions. We have continued contact with many as our "children." This part of our ministry begins with the following story.

Missions in Bangladesh, April, 1998

In 1994, we were called to come to pick up a young lady from the University of Mobile. We were at Dauphin Way Baptist church working in evangelism and reaching out to single adults as well during this time while I was completing my studies in Christian Studies and Organizational Management at University of Mobile until I graduated in 1994, finishing in 1993. The youngest son had started there as a freshman and was in class with Sara, I will use as her name. We learned she had no host family, and immediately she had one. We had already been hosting American students at times, and thus began our international group that continued through the years.

Sara's family had been Christians and in Christian ministry for many years. They invited us to come and do several things. One was a marriage retreat for 23 pastors and wives from the different areas of the country. I was able to preach on a very hot Easter morning out in the open with ministers lining the back of me with over 1600 in attendance with people standing or sitting on the ground. Over 360 came forward that morning accepting Christ.

I was the key speaker for the Bangladesh Baptist Fellowship for that year where there were over a thousand each day in attendance. We enjoyed working with the present International Mission Board missionaries and stayed in the Mission house some of the time, and also we stayed at the home of our friends and missionaries, Tom and Gloria Thurman, who were retiring at the time to return to the states.

We enjoyed being a part of a number of their retirement occasions where we saw God had really endeared them to these people. One such experience was the neighbors next door to them who were not Christians. We listened to their kinds of worship each day, but they loved the Thurmans dearly as all did. When we were about to leave the home of Tom and Gloria, the lady of this family next door came to tell us good by and requested us to please come back and serve where they had been serving. What an honor to us but also to the testimony of these precious friends and as faithful servants for Jesus Christ!

This trip was strenuous for us. The weather was always over 100 degrees day and night with mosquitoes to deal with along with periodic showers during the day and with food not like ours We saw God do some extraordinary miracles while there, especially in our behalf.

Transportation was multiple types on narrow roads. A boat trip for Mary was traumatic as she stood getting on just before the boat left that had over 300 people and built to hold 60. Tom pulled her up to stand on the very last place to stand at the last minute, or she would have been left. We crossed the Ganges River safely arriving at Tom and Gloria's for that part of the 3 weeks there.

I ate some very hot beef prepared by a family for their observance for Ramadan and had traveled by foot, boat, and rickshaw to this house as visitors to accept their hospitality. We saw how the Thurmans were so gracious and truly loved the people developing relationships. This was one occasion with Tom.

I cannot eat spicy food anytime, and especially there. Tom, Gloria, and Mary stood over me that night praying as I was covered in a hot sweat and barely making it. The closest hospital was 80 miles away and hard traveling to get there. We all saw God do a mighty miracle as we have seen Him do multiple times in our lives. We had heard of such stories before of missionaries having difficult times, and heard how God did miracles.

We got to experience them in the form of safety in traveling and recovery from that experience. We had asked specifically for prayer for traveling upon leaving the USA, and while there, we saw why we had felt impelled to pray for that as well as the food area being very different from ours. Mary actually got a parasite from the water on the plane back to the USA. That situation lasted for 3 months trying to figure it out. Tests always said negative. Then she and I contacted the Thurmans to find out what is used to clear it out. We were so happy they knew the medicine which the doctor did prescribe for her. That was the last of it for which we were thankful.

We saw God do wonders at the meeting times, and through the marriage retreat. There were a few couples with difficult marriages. We had purposely planned scriptures for each thought we presented and assured them the Biblical marriage plan did not fit exactly the western style. After 3 days of intense study and group activities, we had them illustrate by art, music, writings, and plays a different concept learned. We were blown away to see the creativeness and the thoughts portrayed showing they had gained understanding of every concept so well.

At the conclusion of the retreat, we had them do a lighting of the Trinity Candle. They prayed for each other, and God restored marriages and further enriched them for years to come. Each pastor was given written material to take back to their areas to teach and lead which gave us much positive feed back for years to come.

For the convention we saw over 1500 attend, and we saw people walk and ride for miles in the heat sleeping on the ground where cobras are known to live. We heard them early in the morning in our "suite" praying for the meetings to be held. A man from the Choke tribe of India had heard of the meeting and wanted to attend some way. He had caught different means to attend and walked also. At the invitation time that first night, he gave his life to Jesus. He wanted to talk to me and told me about his life and his new life he had found. He had heard of this meeting and just knew he had to get to the meeting some way. Somehow he got back home that night and told his wife, whom he brought some way the next morning, because he wanted her to know Jesus.

She accepted Jesus that day also.

Another area we helped was carrying heavy duffle bags full of Christian books on spiritual growth and theology for the seminary that trained pastors. We found it interesting that the Bengali are taught English and Bengali each day. So we were blessed to be able to talk to many people and not have to use a translator some of the time.

This trip was not easy, but God showed us His mighty power in ways we could have never imagined. Truly He is faithful for what He calls us to do for Him.

When we returned from Bangladesh in 1998, I was asked to pastor at Fernwood Baptist Church, Gulfport, MS. This was an hour plus from our home, and Mary stayed in Mobile during the week until end of January, 1999, when she had had time to train another director. While away from our home, we continued to use our home for college students. The youngest son was one by then.

When we went to Fernwood, we found the church very low in attendance. We focused on developing leaders and reaching people for Jesus. The baptistry had not been used in years, but it was cleaned and used almost weekly for the time when we were there. We increased to two morning services. We saw God bring in over 50 into the membership, many with salvation and baptism.

Missions in Indianapolis, IN area

In 2000, we joined DaySpring Baptist Church, Mobile, AL, which was a new church plant. Bro. Darrell had retired from the Mission Board and begun his own ministry, Total Church Life. He served as co-pastor for this new church plant a couple of years, and Bro. Darrell and I both served as Evangelism and Missions pastors. That summer, we took a mission team to the church his youngest son, Loren, pastored, New Faith Community Church, in New Palestine, IN, which was a new church plant sponsored by the North American Mission Board. Here we got to do VBS and other mission activities to help build that church. We went back to help there in the summer of 2001 thus continuing our USA missions effort away from Mobile. Mary enjoyed being the director of the Children's Choir program at Dayspring that included 4 age groups. In the spring of 2001, she organized and presented a musical called, "Nick at Night.

The Beginning of Missions to Brazil

The following stories relate to our Brazilian experiences that began with the next experience. This trip was the first of over 30 that I have had. It was my joy and privilege to take a number of people with me on trips. Pastor

Len Chilton, another *Total Church Life* trainer, went on one with me. As has been true of these going, each had a life-changing experience. Some of these experiences of God's faithfulness I have chosen to share.

Two weeks after 911, Kathy and Mary put Bro. Darrell and me on one of the first planes to leave Mobile on our way to Brazil about Sept. 25, 2001. Bro. Darrell and I traveled to a number of cities and 4 different states in 5 weeks time. We taught the book *The Church as the Storehouse of Gifts*, which title was a translation from Portuguese. The title in Portuguese is *Sues Maravilhoses Dons*, but was originally *Igreja: Celeiro de Dons*. We taught this in seminaries, pastor's conferences, a pastor's retreat, Baptist associational offices, and State Baptist offices. The Brazilian Baptist Convention asked Bro. Darrell to write this book for people there to understand the Christian's spiritual gifts because of the misunderstanding people had about spiritual gifts. There we began our mission together as partners for teaching pastors and church leaders the dynamics and logistics of church growth and development. We used his written materials: *People Sharing Jesus,* and *Total Church Life* as our main sources but also included his other books at different times on other trips. His books, *The Doctrine of Salvation* and the booklet for new Christians, *What's Next*, were other books he wrote.

From DaySpring, we joined Dr. Rick Cagle, at Crosspoint Church in 2002-2003, which was a new church plant as well, where I served as co-pastor in charge of evangelism. It was there that Bro. Rick had a vision of incorporating Evergreen Missions under his umbrella of Evergreen Ministries, Inc. which later became Rick Cagle Ministries, Inc. (In 2012, Bro. Rick went to be with Jesus suddenly. It was a short time later that we established our own ministry, Morton Christian Ministries, Inc.)

We enjoyed forming 2 trips to Brazil in 2002 and then had 2 planned for 2003. The ones in 2002 were so special where we got to do services at churches, VBS type gatherings, and work in some of the social service areas which were owned by the International Mission Board at that time under the direction of the missionary there, Margaret Johnson.

We also went to schools to speak and Mary, some pastors and I went up to Monkey Mountain where we saw poverty. People live in the caves of the mountains. There was a community center which was a social program on top of the mountain directed by a lady and member of the Fellowship Baptist Church where I spoke. She invited me to come up and speak. I had Lucy as my translator. There were so many people that came they could not all come into the building. Many people were saved that night.

A lady who had made a decision for Christ, when I was introducing the pastors, came up and said to me that she and some people could not come on this side of the mountain. I told her that the God I serve is the God of both sides of the mountain.

Bro. Rick and 2 of his children, high school or college age, along with the other team members went to another church where Bro. Rick was preaching. His son, David, presently pastor of The Steeple, one campus of Cottage Hill Baptist Church, Mobile, Alabama, was a team member twice.

We had a wonderful first trip in 2003 with much of the same work as done before in 2002. The churches served and the people have become some of our lifelong friends in those areas. They encourage us as we seek to encourage them. On other later trips, we have had contact as well.

Mary had been teaching in some private and Christian schools for high school and the last one in an elementary one. We were preparing for our second trip to Brazil in 2003 when Mary had a heart attack 2 days before leaving with a team of 10 I was leading. The heart attack was followed by a stroke 4 days later leaving her paralyzed. That trip was cancelled until the summer of 2004. God worked a miracle so that no tickets were lost except for one team member who could not go in 2004. Mary's ticket was redeemed by a niece of hers. Actually the team increased in 2004.

In Mary's situation, we saw God work miracles also. She got a stent on that Wednesday morning of July 9, and we thought that was all there was to it giving the team (many had arrived in Mobile already) clearance to go on with Bobby leading it. Her sister was able to come and assist Mary.

However, on the 10th, we learned Mary had blood clots in arteries and veins, an unknown medical phenomenon. and one clot had caused her arm to become immobile. The only thing they could do was to put multiple blood thinners in her body to counter these which caused a brain bleed causing full paralysis on Saturday, July 12 at 10:00 P.M. At 2:15 A.M., the doctors had told me and Mary's sister that she would not live until morning. At 11 A.M. that Sunday, a heart filter was placed below her heart for any future blood clots, to protect her. But God is still working miracles! The translator, Lucy, in Brazil did not call off the meeting for the team to be attending at the church that Saturday night. They held a 7 hour prayer meeting that we believe saved Mary's life along with the many other people all over the world praying.

When Lucy, our translator and onsite coordinator, called me at 10:00 that Saturday night, I was home preparing to preach that Sunday morning.

Lucy told me Mary was going to be ok because the people met at the church expecting to see the team and learned what had happened. They had held a 7 hour prayer meeting in Mary's behalf. Then I got a call from Nancy, her sister, telling me her body had crashed. I jumped in the car wondering what God was doing and what was going to be the outcome. The Lord intervened through all this with Mary coming home from the 2 hospitals after 25 days. At the one for rehabilitation, she had gotten the use of language and some mobility back. After getting home from hospital, the youngest son, Earnest, really encouraged her to start playing the piano again to hasten the use of her hands, arms, and coordination skills. That was helpful for her recovery of their use as well, and she went back as the pianist at the church where I was the newly called pastor not long before all this happened.

After 2 months, she saw the neurologist who had said at the outset that if she lived, she would be a vegetable. He was so baffled with all her responses to his tests, he could not talk when she came to his office. He was the only non-believer of all the doctors who were so kind and helpful and remain that way to this day. The neurologist dismissed Mary that day; she had walked in, but only with a cane. She performed all the needed tests and was released from him. We pray God used this to affect him spiritually, a purpose we have prayed God would use with others witnessing God's faithfulness in this situation. At future doctor visits, the doctors would tell those around Mary and me that Mary was a walking miracle, and that they had nothing to explain why she lived, except it was a God thing.

Mary went back as the Director of the International Language School in January, 2004, but she felt she needed my help some. This was not unusual as we have always worked as a team in most locations. We worked together in that capacity for a number of years seeing God work miracles in the lives of international students, setting up more sites for the school location, training teachers and staff, and developing longterm relationships with some students with whom we still have contact. During these times of serving as International Language School Director (Mary as my assistant now), I served as interim International Ministries Director twice before being elected during the third interim as Director in Sept., 2015, where I served for 4 1/2 years.

During this time of the ministry with the Mobile Baptist Association, I was asked in August of 2004 to form and pastor a new church plant in the Native American community of Mobile Baptist Association, Shalom Baptist Church which was constituted in October, 2004. Rev. Glenn Vernon, retired as the Director of Camp Whispering Pines in the Citronelle area of Mobile Baptist Association, was also serving part-time as the missionary to the Native American community near the camp. With his leadership, he helped the church get the property as a gift. He was also a great encourager for this ministry until he died. Volunteers helped us clear the property for the building, and some later joined Shalom.

We met in homes at the beginning and until the church building was started in the spring of 2006. We met in the pavilion part as it was being built. A sister church in the area, Lockler Memorial, sponsored and housed us for the first 18 months. During those 18 months, Mary was busy doing Bible clubs weekly each month in 3 different homes getting the people connected to our ministry.

With the help of many churches in the USA, Shalom was built, and the first building and the second building were fully paid for with no debt ever. During those years, mission teams and church partnerships were made, not to just to give financially, but to help build the church physically. Teams came to do VBS and revivals, block parties, ladies meetings, and prayer walks periodically. Volunteers helped from the area as well. Mary and I saw God's faithfulness the whole time we were there. Two special pastors helped so much. Youth pastor, Mike Noles, from north AL, came the first summer with 90 in that mission team meeting under the pavilion of the soon to be building for the church dedicated on the last Sunday of October, 2006. Pastor Mike, later at Launch Point Church in the Shoals area there, came with his youth teams for many years until I left in 2015.

Another pastor, Rev. Ken Jernigan, then at Cresthill Baptist Church in Savanah, GA, came three times with some of the team doing Sports camps and other community projects. On one trip, some adults in the team helped to do inside finishing on the first building. On another trip they framed the second building that became the classrooms and fellowship area. One summer we took the Shalom youth to the Savanah church to do a missions endeavor for them.

Mary was the pianist and led in the presentations of seasonal musicals/dramas she created with all ages participating We had friends to serve in the music and children's areas sometimes. We also had the blessing of several youth leaders, most of those being local college students. One also served as a music leader while with us. Early on we had 2 of our college age Brazilian family members working here for a time that served in the music area. They played other musical instruments along with Mary at the piano while they led the congregation in music. A former International Mission Board missionary young lady served as a volunteer with us also for 9 months, working in the ladies ministry as her focus, but she also served in music, youth, or children's areas as needed. She remains a close friend and encourager today. We are so grateful for how God provided what we needed when we needed it.

We got to see many souls saved and serving Jesus during those number of years there. We praise God that Shalom is still a fully functioning church. While there, we had prayed for the Lord to call a pastor who lived and worked in the area since we knew we would not be there always and lived 35 miles away. God is always faithful to our prayers as we pray in His will. Now the young pastor, Rev. Ray Johnson, was called as pastor in 2019, a fruit of the youth ministry when we began ministry in that area.

God has done an amazing work in his life fitting him so well to serve Jesus there where he still lives and works. His grandparents we had met earlier, Duggar and Alberta Lofton, had been the ones who contacted me to begin a new church plant in that area. They had prayed that God would raise up someone and prayed the church would be filled, especially with their family. Mr. Duggar went home to Heaven early on, but Mrs. Alberta remained faithful serving however she could. She got to see those prayers answered in many ways, including this grandson being her pastor until her death in fall of 2021. Again, God proved His faithfulness to these dedicated and caring two people in seeing so much realized from their prayers.

When I retired from the Director of International Ministries in October of 2019, I was called as pastor several months earlier to revitalize Smithtown Baptist Church near our home. I was there until March of 2022 when I had to retire due to the ongoing health issues I had had for a year. During these years, we got to see God bless and bring increase to the membership with believers joining and many with profession of faith and baptism. We had the joy of having international friends periodically in the services, and two families joined.

The college age youth and children's ministry leaders the church called helped us develop those areas so much, and in 2021, I took 3 of the high school young men with me on a mission trip to New Orleans with Youth Pastor, Mike Noles, our partner from days at Shalom. Bro. Mike was helpful with youth weekends for our youth at Smithtown. (Our own youth leaders led some awesome weekend times as well and weekly gatherings.) The 3 young men enjoyed working in deprived areas with Bro. Mike's team and made such great contributions to those reached. We praise God for all He did during the 4 years we served at Smithtown.

Bro. Darrell and I went to Brazil together a number of times, but most of my over 30 mission trips to Brazil I led. During the 13 years of pastoring at Shalom and those at Smithtown, I was taking mission trips to Brazil and went to Puerto Rico 5 times.

On 4 different trips to Brazil, Bro. Darrell and I were working together on projects for the Brazilian Baptist Convention. One trip was a special opportunity in which we were asked to teach pastors and church leaders the *People Sharing Jesus* book during Carnival (Mardi Gras here). Typically in Brazil, churches go to retreats during Carnival. Using the techniques from People Sharing Jesus, the people connected with people during Carnival to share Jesus.

On one of the Wednesdays, we stopped at the church where I was to speak about witnessing. The state evangelism director, Bro. Darrell, and I saw that the Carnival was coming down the street next to the church. The three of us handed out tracts as the pastor blocked the door to the church. When the Carnival was completed, the people returned to us and asked us what this tract meant. We had the opportunity to divide up the people between the three of us and lead many people to the Lord. The pastor was very upset with us about what we did because he saw that Carnival was so evil.

After church, we drove on to the conference center where there was a large gathering of pastors and church leaders. We taught them Thursday, Friday, and Saturday the book, *People Sharing Jesus*. Surprisingly, the pastor where we were Wednesday night, showed up Thursday morning. Saturday afternoon, Bro. Darrell asked me what we should do Saturday night. My suggestion, after I found out they were having a large Carnival at the city square that evening, was that we take our equipment to our room. Then take the table we had used for equipment and stack it up with tracts.

When the people arrived for the evening session, Bro. Darrell opened with prayer and had me go to the front to tell the people what we would be doing for Saturday night. We told them we all would be putting into practice what we had been studying for the last several days by going to the carnival and witnessing. That night many people came to know Jesus. I told them this was like catching fish in a barrel because there were many people gathered up around the city square which provided a block of opportunities. The pastor that was opposed to the carnival witnessing came up to me on Sunday after the service and asked for forgiveness. He said he was going back to the church and the Sunday night service the people would be going to the Carnival. He told me how God had used us to change his heart about Carnival.

Now this pastor is using that time as a witnessing opportunity.

Subsequently, when doing future teaching on our trips, this manner of teaching witnessing in Carnival was used to reach more people for Jesus. Many churches then turned this time from retreats to evangelistic efforts.

I asked some of our translators in Brazil to include some of their observations and influences of these trips where they helped us. You will see these testimonials later. We appreciate them so much as they were the link to the people as we shared. Bro. Darrell and I developed enough Portuguese through the years to teach, preach, and converse with people some, but we greatly relied on our translators the most.

Some years ago as Bro. Darrell and I were in a church

in western Brazil, we taught church leaders and pastors about church strategy. After we had completed our teaching, a young lady came asking me if I would visit her husband while there, and I agreed. I had a translator go with me to make that visit. When I arrived, I was greeted by her young husband who was huge. His first comment was, "You have fifteen minutes and then I want you out of here." He let me know how much he hated the church, the people that went to church, God Himself, and wanted nothing to do with the church. Soon into our conversation, he began to open up about his abuse as a child in a church school. He soon had some questions for me, and I used Scripture to answer his questions. Before long, this monster of a guy who was filled with anger and hate surrendered his life to Christ and was filled with joy and peace. Later I found out that he had said he would kill any preacher who stepped foot on his property. So much for that as I watched this man transformed by the love of our Lord. God is faithful.

Another account happened as I was teaching in one of the churches in Rio. The pastor received a phone call from the top drug kingpin who heard about an American speaking at the church. He wanted me to come to his house on top of the mountain. Two pastors warned me how dangerous it would be to make that visit. We prayed and I had a peace about making that visit. We made the long steep journey to his house and had a wonderful visit. I shared the gospel with him, and I prayed for him and with him. A short time later he accepted Jesus and got his education at the seminary. I met up with one of those pastors who told me what happened after our visit of how God had called him into the ministry. He is now pastoring one of the fastest growing churches and reaching his old drug dealers for Christ.

In Brasilia, I was asked to go visit one of the military officials. His nephew was my translator while in Brasilia. He asked me to go with him to visit his uncle. He was a very hard hearted person, and when we arrived at his home, he met us at the door and was trying to hold his two small dogs. When I sat down on the couch, the dogs got down and came to get in my lap. He said these dogs had NEVER had anything to do with anyone but their immediate family.

He could not understand how or why those dogs were in my lap. They had never done that before. Generally, they would keep barking at the different people around him. I told him that was ok because I enjoyed his dogs and missed our dog. I showed him a picture of our dog, and he said, "Oh, you are a dog person." I said, "Yes." The dogs played and loved on me the whole time we were there.

I began sharing with him about why we had come to visit. As I was sharing, he said in a very harsh voice, "Stop." He got up and left the room and came back with his family. He said, "Now, go ahead." Again, he said stop when I began talking. He went out and got his teenage children's friends who were visiting his children. When they were all there, he said he wanted them to listen to what I had to say.

Each one listened as I shared. He and his family and the friends of his children all accepted Christ but one. We found out that one was a Christian already. We think sometimes that distractions can be a hindrance but can be a help. God used those dogs to make an inroad to share with all of them. This shows God's faithfulness no matter the circumstances when we want to love and serve him. It rewarded the nephew in his faithfulness to keep praying and asking God to help his family to know Jesus. This outcome proves we are to keep on praying never knowing when and how God will answer our prayers. We just don't give up being faithful to persevere in prayer. Galatians 6:9 reveals this truth: Let us not grow weary for doing good, for in due season, we shall reap if we do not lose heart.

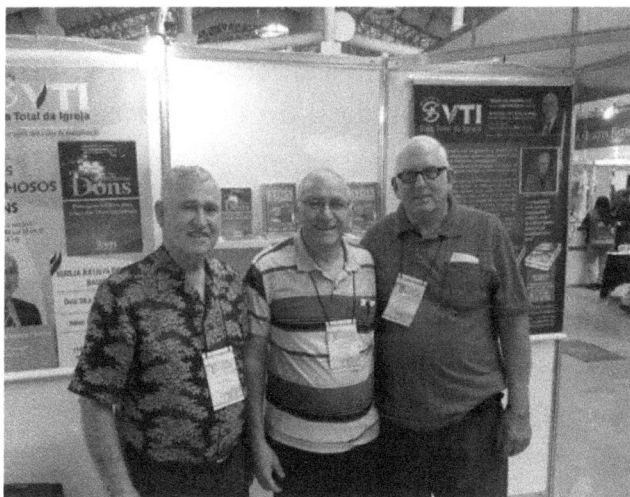

Belem, 2017; Left to right: Dr. Darrell Robinson, Pr. Odilon Pereira, Dr. Bobby Morton. Odilon serves as Total Church Life coordinator for Brazil.

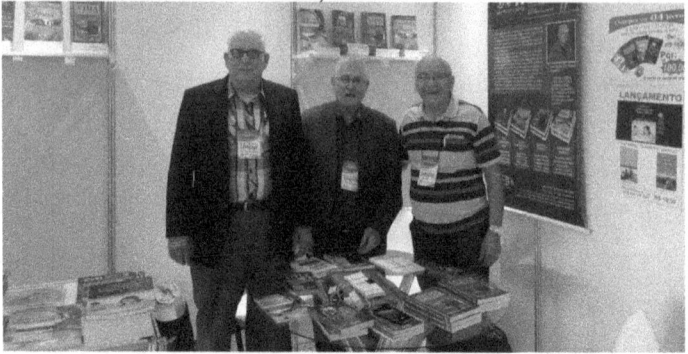

Pocos de Caldas, Brazil, 2018

Experiences in a South Asian Country

Due to the location, I will only say a few things. Bro. Darrell and I were invited to come to this area to teach pastors. We found, while there, that God has a sense of humor.

The pastors were afraid that the Taliban were going to blow up the hotel we were staying in. It just so happened that the top governmental officials were staying in the hotel where we were staying. The top official was in the room next to me. They had armed guards from the military guarding the hotel for miles around. They even offered for me to bring my entire family there to teach English as a Second Language.

I had a driver that drove me wherever I needed to go. He was very committed to the world religion he was involved in. On the very last night of our stay, he had driven me to the church where I spoke. In returning to the hotel, we got into a discussion about Christianity. That night, with tears running down his cheek, he bowed his head and accepted Christ. I told him to talk to the people at the church where he had taken me about his decision. I pray he became a staunch follower of Jesus. Sometimes you share, but you may not know the results of that sharing. That is when you leave the results to Jesus and trust for His omnipotent power and faithfulness to prevail.

Experiences in northern India

Bro. Darrell and I were invited to teach at this seminary two full classes to be done in 9 days that normally runs for a semester. That meant very long days and nights for the students and us.

After training and during a break one afternoon, we all went out into the streets to witness and practice what they had learned which is the practical aspect of the training anywhere. We saw many people come to Christ. The students were energized by seeing how God will work through their lives to touch others' lives for Christ. This was a tremendous blessing for the pastors to see the excitement in the students and an answer to our prayers.

India, 2015

One of My Last Trips to Brazil Before Covid

I was invited to go to teach the *People Sharing Jesus* in a very large church in southern Brazil. We had hundreds attend each day and night. On Saturday, over 200 came to go house to house witnessing. It was amazing that each one going reached at least one person for Christ. We came back to the church and shared with the church. Sunday morning I preached and the pastor translated for me who had pastored for a number of years in the USA. He was very fluent in American English.

When the invitation was given, over 165 people came giving their hearts to Jesus. The pastor and I agreed that that had been a God thing. Also some of the people that had made a decision on Saturday attended the worship service as well, and they came forward also. This gives evidence that when we are faithful and doing His will, He rewards our faithfulness.

That Sunday night I was in a very large church in that city and saw God move in the same kind of way with about the same number of decisions. Some students that had been visitors from Brazil in our home were in attendance that night, and the young ladies and their parents made decisions for Christ that night. That was a very rewarding experience for me personally helping me and the team realize that we never know when seeds are planted that they will grow to fruition.

Significant Experiences from Our Translators from Brazil

From: Ligia Vieira de Araujo Hasse

It was my privilege to translate for Bobby on three of his mission trips. They included Sao Paulo (Guarulhos), Rio de Janeiro (Teresopolis), and Parana (Curitiba). I recall seeing them share, translating, and watching how God brought great results. The times were in services, classes, or personal witness with others.

We had many experiences teaching People Sharing Jesus, but the most memorable ones are those I watched and helped when we were out on the streets talking with people. One memory I cherish is the day we visited people in a favela (translated slums) in Rio. Dr. Steve Bailey, a fellow pastor and friend, was with Bobby this time. Bobby had such a positive impact as a foreign pastor there as did Steve. That community really felt special that day as we saw Bobby's life bless them and show God's love.

The way Bobby approaches people to share Jesus is what impresses me the most. Through God's direction, he always finds the best way to connect with people and get them to listen to what the Holy Spirit inspires him to say.

From Luciana Matos

My story with Pastor Bobby and Mary-

I have always wanted to be a missionary and work in the work of God. I prayed and asked God about how I could do something in my profession that would allow me to work in missions, have my livelihood, and still contribute directly to missions.

And so it was to be. I started studying English at the age of 14, and when I was 16, I met Pastor Bobby and his wife. They had come to Brazil on a mission trip and were in front of a group of people showing people here how to win souls for Jesus. How to translate and work with them changed my life! Since then we have been on missions in Rio de Janeiro and Sao Paulo.

I would like to report on two special moments I witnessed with Pr. Bobby. The first one I remember was being in my church, translating the word of God that Pr. Bobby was presenting, and throughout the presentation, and the people he had spoken to during the day were coming. More people were arriving until the place was crowded with people thirsty for the word of God.

And His presence of our heavenly Father was something indescribable!

At another time, we were walking through one of the most dangerous places in Rio de Janeiro, the Favela of Jacarezinho. We met thieves, drug dealers, prostitutes, and they all heard of the way to know Jesus and were touched by the presence of God through the life of Pr. Bobby. It was a tremendous thing to see God's action and how Pr. Bobby led the gospel and led people to the feet of Christ.

Pr. Bobby Morton and his dear wife became special people in my life, something that goes beyond translation. With Bobby and Mary, I learned a lot from God, from His word, and gained two people I love so much in this life. My gratitude goes to God for knowing both, and today they are part of my life.

From Jonatas Bento:

What a wonderful blessing it has been working with Pastor Bobby Morton throughout the years since meeting him in 2002.

I accepted Christ through an American missionary when I was a teenager. Since that time, I started studying English in order to offer myself as a volunteer for other American missionaries to spread the Word in Brazil and other nations.

Working with Pastor Bobby is very easy and simple just like working with and for Jesus; walking along several streets, knocking on doors going door to door, sharing the Gospel and giving a word of comfort and the plan of salvation to each citizen who was open to hear the Word of God.

When I ask myself, "What would Jesus do?", I have the answer that Pastor Bobby follows exactly our Master's directions, teaching and sharing the love of our Almighty God to every creature on earth.

Indeed, God has been faithful to different generations in several parts of the world where He sent His warrior to fight against all evil and to share His love with every one. I hope many others have the same chance I had to meet a true pastor with a true love in his heart for lost souls.

FROM THE AUTHOR'S HEART

The Lord laid this work on my heart while Bro. Darrell and I were teaching in Brazil. I began this writing as a commentary for the book of Joshua. After I had started this book as above, I had some mixed feelings about this. My wife and Bro. Darrell were on the same page to change this from a commentary to a devotional style book.

I stopped my writing for a while, and as I prayed through their suggestions, I felt God leading me to change this to a devotional style writing. That meant I had to start all over. It is my prayer that this book will be an encouragement to each reader.

As I have traveled and been in so many churches in the USA and around the world, one of the things that I have noticed is how discouraged so many people are in the church today. Our world is filled with so much negativism that is felt around world.

I remember when Evangelist Freddie Gage came to Mobile, AL for a crusade a number of years ago for a pastors' training in preparation for the crusade, and made this statement: "I see more life in the mortuary at midnight than I do in the average church." Scriptures tell us to be filled with overflowing joy. Yet there are more frowns than smiles.

I realize that people have unwanted circumstances in their lives. As Christians, we cannot allow life situations to defeat us and allow Satan to steal our joy. When unwanted circumstances do come, as Christians we have the peace that passes all understanding that can heal our hearts and gives us hope for the future.

In John 10:10, the Scripture tells us that the thief comes to steal, kill and destroy. Then Jesus said, "I have come that you can have life and life more abundantly."

The way we choose to deal with our circumstances, be they whatever, is up to us to look to Jesus for strength in the trials and grief, and to give Jesus praise for the blessings that we have to enjoy. May we be encouraged that Jesus has already overcome the things in this world and is victorious. In Christ, we are victors as well.

For example, as I finish this book, I am taking a second round of medicine by infusion to remove this lymphoma. The first months did not completely remove it, and I know we have more tests and trials to go to get past this, whatever is His plan. I am praying for healing, have seen His hand of healing in many ways through our prayers and the prayers of people around the world. I want to be with family longer and serve Jesus.

However, while I have been in the hospital the past year and in these clinics for infusion and medical assistance, I am always overcome and amazed by how God is using these places, even in this state, to try to encourage others, even Christians. Mary and I together feel so privileged that God would allow us to keep being used regardless of our circumstances.

For example, while I was trying to finish the book for the publisher, this has been one of those days with sharing with volunteers, staff, and medical personnel telling things in our lives and them sharing things with us of things in their lives, some good things and some not good. All of this has been an encouragement to us while seeking to encourage them.

Some of you reading may not be sure of your salvation because you cannot point back to a day knowing that upon this day is the day that you accepted Christ. If you are wondering today, the Bible says in Romans 10:9: "If you confess with your mouth the Lord Jesus, and believe in your heart that God raised Him from the dead, you will be saved." You can now settle that today by praying a simple prayer like this:

Lord, I thank you for loving me, for dying for me. I ask you now to forgive me of my sins and to come into my heart to be my Lord and Savior. I thank you for loving me, for dying on the cross for me, and I now ask you to come into my life to be my Lord and Savior. Thank you for giving me eternal life.

Please contact me so that you can begin to grow in Christ. Email me at drremorton@comcast.net and follow us on Facebook @Morton Christian Ministries.

Give me your number, and we can talk. I will be more than glad to talk and encourage you.

ACKNOWLEDGEMENTS

I want to thank my wife for her love, support and assistance to get this book in print. God gave me Mary as a special helpmate to be at my side to support me in ministry and every area of life. I believe this is one of the major purposes He spared her life in 2003.

A very special thing in all my trips has been that she puts an envelope in my checked bag with individual envelopes with scriptures and prayers dated for each day that I have been gone, and we were not together. The first thing I did each morning was to get that and read one in my devotional time

When Bro. Darrell and I were together, the first thing he wanted me to do was for me to read the one for that day. On one of our trips, he became very sick. The one, for that morning following the night he got sick, was a scripture about health, and her prayer was for our health. We both reflected upon how many times Mary had sent scriptures and prayer thoughts that met the exact needs for that day. One of her main emphasis in life is her prayer life.

She reminded me of a special moment related to a

time I was doing a conference in Shocco Springs Baptist Assembly. Mary and I had the opportunity to serve as Special Consultants for the Alabama Baptist State Board of Missions for over 15 years teaching people across the state how to grow the Bible study time on Sunday mornings or whenever meeting.

I had mentioned that each teacher should be praying for the class members' salvation. A lady teaching the oldest ladies class of 80 to 90 year olds got very upset with me. She came up to tell me that she had been teaching these ladies for years, and each one had a special chair for meeting times. I posed the question, "But have you prayed for each and know that each one is saved?" At this time, she got very upset with me and walked away.

A year later I was teaching another conference at Shocco again when I spotted her coming to me. I was somewhat apprehensive to greet her.

She came to tell me that what I had said really bore into her making her to really concentrate on if each was saved. She told me that after she had started praying and talking with each one, that 3 acknowledged Jesus as Savior, and she asked me to pray for a fourth one. The ladies had never talked in the class, but after God started working in their lives, she had not been able to get in very much teaching. They were just so excited to tell how Jesus was working in their lives and using them.

Mary and I have always focused on praying in each area we minister and for each person where we minister. If we want to see God at work and experience His faithfulness, prayer has to be the first and most important ingredient for success.

Mary is a very gifted writer herself and has some published articles and 2 books. The last one came out in April of 2022 entitled: *Single, But Not Alone....And Then*. The first part of the recent book was written and published in 1981 when she was single, and it was reprinted in 2022. The present one includes this earlier story, but also our meeting each other, and gives a brief overview of how God has used us in certain types of ministry. The book is listed as Mary Strebeck Morton, author, published by this publisher and is available on the internet by the major book distributors, but also it can be found through Walmart.

Also I want to thank my children: Chris, Bobbi Morton Smith, Earnest, and their spouses, along with our 7 grandchildren and our 8 great grandsons who have given me immeasurable love and support. I have had the privilege and blessing of taking some of my children and grand children plus some of our extended family members on mission trips to Brazil, a true joy for me. Also my thanks goes to our now deceased parents and extended families for their prayers and love through the years.

My sister-in-law, Nancy Strebeck, has been a great encourager and assistant in helping me to get started, especially by giving her expertise and recommendations as a retired college English professor. When we have had needs physically or on mission trips, she has been faithful to provide caregiving to our furry family members as we had them, and to take care of us also when we had physical needs. She truly has a servant's heart.

I want to say thank you to the multitude of friends

gathered through the years, church families, and fellow laborers in ministry that have greatly encouraged us in our ministry and difficult circumstances, especially through their prayers. They are too numerous to mention by name.

I cannot say enough for my appreciation to my friend and mentor, Dr. Darrell Robinson. This is a tribute to him as well. I regret his health failed before he could tell much himself about his many experiences in travel worldwide, but I pray that you can see how his invaluable influence and encouragement has been so beneficial for me. It has been my joy to partner with him on many occasions in the USA and other countries teaching how to share the love of Jesus and grow a church spiritually. We were so in tune with each other that one of us could just stop, and the other would keep the teaching going not missing a beat. Truly my life has been so enriched, and I am privileged to have been his friend and partner in ministry.

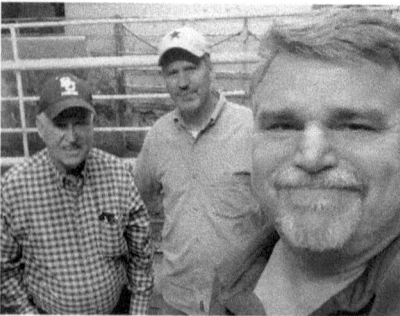

Bro. Darrell, sons Robin and Loren.
Robin is presently the Director for Total Church Life.
His contact number is 281-755-7954

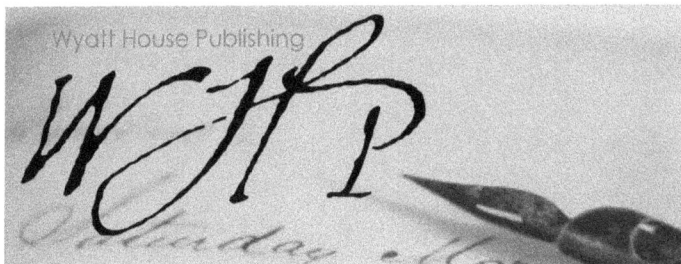

Wyatt House Publishing

You have a story.
We want to publish it.

Everyone has as a story to tell. It might be about something you know how to do, or what has happened in your life, or it may be a thrilling, or romantic, or intriguing, or heartwarming, or suspenseful story, starring a cast of characters that have been swimming around in your imagination.

And at Wyatt House Publishing, we can get your story onto the pages of a book just like the one you are holding in your hand. With professional interior design and a custom, professionally designed cover built just for you from the start, you can finally see your dream of being an author become reality. Then, you will see your book listed with retailers all over the world as people are able to buy your book from wherever they are and have it delivered to their home or their e-reader.

So what are you waiting for? This is your time.

visit us at

www.wyattpublishing.com

for details on how to get started becoming a
published author right away.